A Russian Schoolboy

A Russian Schoolboy

Sergei Aksakov

Translated by J. D. Duff

Paul Dry Books

Philadelphia   2009

First Paul Dry Books Edition, 2009

First published in Russia in 1856
under the title *Vospominaniia*.

Paul Dry Books, Inc.
Philadelphia, Pennsylvania
www.pauldrybooks.com

1 3 5 7 9 8 6 4 2
Printed in the United States of America

Library of Congress Cataloging-in-Publication Data
Aksakov, S. T. (Sergei Timofeevich), 1791–1859.
   [Vospominaniia. English]
   A Russian schoolboy / Sergei Aksakov ; translated by J. D. Duff.
— 1st Paul Dry Books ed.
      p. cm.
   Continues: Years of childhood.
   ISBN 978-1-58988-051-1 (alk. paper)
   1. Aksakov, S. T. (Sergei Timofeevich), 1791–1859—Childhood
and youth. 2. Authors, Russian—19th century—Biography.
I. Duff, J. D. (James Duff), 1860–1940. II. Title.
   PG3321.A5Z513 2009
   891.73'3—dc22
   [B]
                                          2008030467

Contents

1

⌘

My First Term at School

In the middle of winter in the year 1799, when I was eight years old, we traveled to Kazan, the chief town of the Province. The frost was intense; and it was a long time before we could find out the lodgings we had taken beforehand. They consisted of two rooms in a small house belonging to a Mme. Aristov, the wife of an officer; the house stood in Georgia Street, a good part of the town. We arrived towards evening, traveling in a common sledge of matting drawn by three of our own horses harnessed abreast; our cook and a maid had reached Kazan before us. Our last stage was a long one, and we drove about the town for some hours in quest of our lodgings, with long halts caused by the stupidity of our country servants—and I remember that I was chilled to the bone, that our lodgings were cold, and that tea failed to warm me; when I went to bed, I was shaking like a man in a fever. I remember also that my mother who loved me passionately was shivering too, not with cold but with fear that her darling child, her little Seryozha, had caught a chill. She pressed me close to her heart, and laid over our coverlet a satin cloak lined with fox-fur that had been part of her dowry. At last I got warm and went to sleep; and next morning I woke up quite well, to the inexpressible joy of my anxious mother. My sister and brother, both younger than I, had been left behind with our father's aunt, at her house of Chufarovo in the Province of Simbirsk. It was expected that we should inherit her property; but for the present she would not give a penny to my father, so that he and his family were pretty often in difficulties; she was unwilling even to lend him a single ruble. I do not know the circumstances which induced my parents, straitened as they were for money, to travel to Kazan; but I do know that it was not done on my account, though my whole future was affected by this expedition.

When I awoke next morning, I was much impressed by the movement of people in the street; it was the first time I had seen anything of the kind, and the impression was so strong that I could not tear myself away from the window. Our maid, Parasha, who had come with us, could not satisfy me by her replies to my questions, for she knew as little as I did; so I managed to get hold of a maid belonging to the house and went on for some hours teasing her with questions, some of which she was puzzled to answer. My father and mother had gone off to the Cathedral to pray there, and to some other places on business of their own; but they refused to take me, fearing for me the intense cold of that Epiphany season. They dined at home, but drove out again in the evening. Tired out by new sensations, I fell asleep earlier than usual, while chattering myself and hearing Parasha chatter. But I had hardly got to sleep when the same Parasha roused me with a kind and careful hand; and I was told that a sledge had been sent for me, and I must get up at once and go to a party where I should find my parents. I was dressed in my best clothes, washed, and brushed; then

I was wrapped up and placed in the sledge, still in Parasha's company. I was naturally shy; I had been caught up out of the sound sleep of childhood and was frightened by such an unheard-of event, so that my heart failed me and—as we drove through the deserted streets of the town—I had a presentiment of something terrible. At last we reached the house. Parasha took off my wraps in the hall and, repeating in a whisper the encouragement she had given me several times on our way, led me to the drawing room, where a footman opened the door and I walked in.

The glitter of candles and sound of loud voices alarmed me so much that I stood stock-still by the door. My father was the first to see me; he called out, "Ah, there is the recruit!"—which alarmed me still more. "Your forehead!" cried someone in a stentorian voice, and a very tall man rose from an armchair and walked towards me. I understood the meaning of this phrase* and was so terrified by it that I turned instinctively to run away, till I was checked by the loud laughter of all the company. But the joke did not amuse my mother: her tender heart was troubled by the fears of her child, and she ran towards me, took me in her arms, and gave me courage by her words and caresses. I shed a few tears but soon grew calm.

And now I must explain where I had been taken. It was the house of an old friend of the family, Maxim Knyazhevich, who, after living for several years at Ufa as my father's colleague in the law courts, had moved with his wife to Kazan, to perform the same duties there. In early youth he had left his native country of Serbia and at once received

* That is, "Present your forehead" to be shaved. In those days the hair on the forehead of recruits for the Army was shaved as soon as they were approved by the doctors.

a commission in the Russian Horse Guards; later he had been sent to Ufa in a legal capacity. He might be called a typical specimen of a Southern Slav, and was remarkable for his cordial and hospitable temperament. As he was very tall and had harsh features, his exterior was at first sight rather disturbing; but he had the kindest of hearts. His wife, Elizabeth, was the daughter of a Russian noble. Their house in Kazan was distinguished by this inscription over the entrance: "Good people, you are welcome"— a true expression of Slav hospitality. When they lived at Ufa, we often met, and my sister and I used to play with the two elder sons, Dmitri and Alexander. The boys were in the room, though I did not recognize them at once; but when my mother explained, and reminded me of them, I called out at once, "Why, mama, surely these are the boys who taught me how to crack walnuts with my head!" The company laughed at my exclamation, my shyness passed off, and in good spirits I began to renew acquaintance with my former playmates. They were dressed in green uniforms with scarlet collars, and I was told that they attended the grammar school of Kazan. An hour later, they drove back to school; it was Sunday, and the two boys had leave to spend the day with their parents till eight in the evening.

I soon grew weary; and, as I listened to the talk between my parents and our hosts, I was falling asleep, when suddenly my ear was caught by some words which filled me with horror and drove sleep far from me. "Yes, my good friends, Alexei Stepanich and Sofya Nikolaevna," M. Knyazhevich was speaking in his loud positive voice, "do take a piece of friendly advice, and send Seryozha to the grammar school here. It is especially important, because I can see that he is his mother's darling, and she will spoil him and coddle him till she makes an old woman of him. It is time for the boy to be learning something; at Ufa the only teacher was Matvei Vasilich at the National School, and he was no great hand; but now that you have gone to live in the country, you won't find anyone even as good." My father said that he agreed entirely with this opinion, but my mother turned pale at the thought of parting with her treasure and replied, with much agitation, that I was still young and weak in health (which was true, to some extent) and so devoted to her that she could not make up her mind in a moment to such a change. As for me, I sat there more dead than alive, neither hearing nor understanding anything further that was said. Supper was served at ten o'clock, but neither my mother nor I could swallow a morsel. At last the same sledge which had brought me carried us back to our lodgings. At bedtime, when I embraced my mother as usual and clung close to her, we both began to sob aloud. My voice was choked, and I could only say, "Mama, don't send me to school!" She sobbed too, and for a long time we prevented my father from sleeping. At last she decided that nothing should induce her to part from me, and towards morning we fell asleep.

We did not stay long at Kazan. I learned afterwards that my father and the Knyazheviches went on urging my mother to send me as a Government scholar* to the school in that town. They pressed upon her that at present there was a vacancy, and there might be none later. But nothing would induce her to give way, and she said positively that she must have a year at least to gain courage, to become accustomed herself and to accustom me to the idea. All this

---

* A boy whose education and maintenance were provided free of charge.

was concealed from me, and I believed that I should never be the victim of such a terrible calamity.

We started on our long journey, taking our own horses, and traveled first to the Province of Simbirsk where we picked up my brother and sister, and then across the Volga to New Aksakovo, where my infant sister, Annushka, had been left. In those days you might travel along side roads in the Province of Ufa for a dozen versts* without passing a single village; and a winter journey of this kind seems to me now so horrible that the mere recollection of it is painful. A side road was merely a track over the snowdrifts, formed by the passage of a few sledges, and the least wind covered it entirely with fresh snow. On such a road the horses had to be harnessed in single file, and the traveler had to crawl on for seven hours without a break, the stages being as much as thirty-five versts or even longer; and the length of each verst was by no means a fixed distance. Hence it was necessary to start at midnight, to wake the children from their sleep, wrap them up in furs, and pack them into the sledges. The creaking of the runners on the dry snow was a constant trial to my nerves, and I always suffered from sickness during the first twenty-four hours. Then the stops for food and sleep, in huts full of smoke and packed with calves and lambs and litters of pigs, the dirt, the smell—Heaven preserve any man from even dreaming of all this! I say nothing of the blizzards which sometimes forced us to halt in some nameless hamlet and wait forty-eight hours till the fierce wind fell. The recollection is bad enough. But we did at last reach my dear Aksakovo, and all was forgotten.

I began once more my life of blissful happiness in my mother's company and resumed all my old occupations. I

---

* A verst is approximately three-quarters of a mile.

read aloud to her my favorite books—*Reading for Children, to Benefit the Heart and Head*, and also *Hippocrene, or the Delights of Literature*—not, indeed, for the first time but always with fresh satisfaction. I recited verses from the tragedies of Sumarokov, in which I had a special preference for messengers' parts, and put on a broad belt for the purpose, with a window-prop stuck in it to represent a sword. I played with my sister whom I had loved dearly from infancy, and my little brother, lying about with them on the floor, which for warmth was covered with a double thickness of snow-white Kalmyck mats. I began again teaching my sister to read, but at first she made slow progress and would not try, and I had naturally little notion how to set about my task, though I was tremendously in earnest over it. I well remember that I found it quite impossible to explain to my six-year-old pupil how to spell whole words. I gave it up in despair, sat down on a stool in the corner, and began to cry. When my mother asked what I was crying about, I answered, "Sister does not understand anything." As before, I took my cat to bed with me; she was so attached to me that she followed me everywhere like a dog; and I snared small birds or trapped them and kept them in a small room which was practically converted into a spacious coop. I admired my pigeons with double tufts and feathered legs, which had been kept warm in my absence under the stoves in the houses of the outdoor servants. I watched the huntsmen catching magpies and pigeons or feeding the hawks in their winter quarters. The day was not long enough for the enjoyment of all these delights!

So winter passed by, and spring began with its green leaves and blossoms, revealing a multitude of new and poignant pleasures—the clear waters of the river, the mill and milldam, the Jackdaw Wood, and the island, surrounded on all sides by the old and new channels of the Buguruslan, and planted with shady limes and birches. I ran to the island several times a day, hardly knowing myself why I went; and there I stood motionless, as if under a spell, while my heart beat hard and my breath came unevenly. But what attracted me most of all was fishing, and I gave my whole soul to this sport, under the eye of my attendant, Yefrem Yevseich. Fish swarmed in the clear, deep waters of the Buguruslan, which flowed right under the windows of the room built on to the old house by my grandfather in his lifetime, in order that his daughter-in-law might have a place to herself to live in. Close under the window there grew a spreading birch, leaning over the water, and one thick crooked bough formed with the trunk a kind of armchair in which I loved to sit with my sister. But the river in the course of time bared the roots of the tree, so that it grew old prematurely and fell on its side; yet it is still living and puts forth leaves. A young tree was planted beside it by a later owner.

Ah, where is it now, that magic world, the fairy tale of human life, which so many grown-up people treat roughly and rudely, shattering its enchantment by ridicule or premature enlightenment? The happiness of childhood is the Golden Age, and the recollection of it has power to move the old man's heart with pleasure and with pain. Happy the man who once possessed it and is able to recall the memory of it in later years! With many, that time passes by unnoticed or unenjoyed, and all that remains in the ripeness of age is the recollection of the coldness or even cruelty of men.

I spent the whole summer in the intoxication of a child's happiness, and suspected nothing; but when autumn came and I began to sit more in the house, to look more at my mother and listen to her more, I soon noticed a change of some kind in her. Her beautiful eyes were directed at me sometimes with a peculiar expression of secret sorrow; I even noticed tears, though they were carefully concealed from me. In grief and excitement, with all the caresses of passionate love, I besieged her with questions. At first she assured me that it was nothing and of no importance, but soon in the course of our conversations, I began to hear her lamenting that I had no proper teacher, and saying that teaching was indispensable for a boy. She would rather die, she said, than see her children grow up in ignorance; a man must serve the state, and was not fit to do so without education. My heart sank when I understood the drift of these words and realized that the dreaded calamity had not passed away but had come close, and that the school at Kazan was inevitable. My mother confirmed my surmise: she said that her mind was made up, and I knew that she did not readily change her resolves. For some days I could only weep, not listening to what she said, and pretending not to understand it. At last her tears and entreaties, her sensible arguments accompanied by the tenderest caresses, and her eager desire to see me grow up an educated man—all these became intelligible to me, young as I was, and I submitted with an aching heart to the destiny that awaited me. But all my country amusements suddenly lost their charm. I felt drawn to none of them; everything seemed to me strange and repulsive, and only my love for my mother increased so much as actually to frighten her.

And now my preparation for the school course began. I could read excellently for my age, but my writing was childish. In arithmetic, my father had tried earlier to impart to me the first four rules, which were all he knew himself; but I was so dull and idle a pupil that he dropped it. Now there was a complete change: in two months I mastered these four rules, and, though I have forgotten all the rest of my mathematics, I remember the four rules still. The rest of the time until our departure for Kazan was spent in revising old lessons with my father. In the writing of copies also I became very proficient. All this I did under my mother's eye and wholly and solely for her sake. She had said that she would burn with shame if I did not pass with credit the entrance examination which had to be taken in these subjects, and that she was sure I would distinguish myself; and I needed no other inducement. I would not go one step from her side. When she tried to send me out to play or look at my pigeons and hawks, I refused to go anywhere and always gave the same answer, "I don't want to, mama." In order to accustom me to the thought of our parting, she spoke constantly to me of the school and of education. She said that she was quite determined to send me to Moscow later, and place me at a boarding school connected with the University, the school to which she had sent her brothers straight from Ufa, when she was herself a girl only seventeen years old. My intelligence was beyond my age; for I had read many books to myself, and still more aloud to my mother, some of them too advanced for my years. To this I must add that my mother was my constant companion, and it is well known how the companionship of grown-up people develops the minds of children. Hence it came about that she was able to speak to me of the advantages the educated have over the ignorant and that I was able to understand her. She was remarkably intelligent and had unusual powers of expression; she could speak what was in her mind with a passion which it was hard to resist, and her influence over me was absolute and supreme. At last she inspired me with such courage, such zeal to carry out her darling wish as soon as possible and justify her hopes, that I even looked forward with impatience to our jour-

ney to Kazan. My mother seemed courageous and cheerful, but how much the effort cost her! She grew thinner
and paler daily; she never shed tears, but she shut herself
up in her own room more than usual and prayed. This was
the real proof of her love for her child, the real triumph of
that infinitely disinterested and self-sacrificing passion! As
a child, I had been long ill, and there was a time when for
whole years she had never left my bedside; when she slept,
no one knew, and no hand but hers was suffered to touch
me. And again, at a later time, when she heard that I had
broken down at school and was lying sick in the hospital,
she crossed the river Kama at the time of the spring thaw,
when all traffic over it had ceased and the discolored and
swollen ice might be expected to break up at any moment.
But all this falls short of her determination to send her child
to school; the school was under the Government and four-
hundred versts away, and the child, whom she literally idol-
ized, was only eight and not strong and had been tenderly
reared; yet she did it, because there was no other means of
procuring an education for him.

Winter came round once more, and in December we
started for Kazan. In order that the return home might be
less sad for my mother, my father insisted on taking my
elder sister with us; my brother and younger sister were
left at home with our aunt Tatyana. At Kazan we had the
same lodgings as the year before, in the house of Mme.
Aristov. Before leaving, my parents had been in correspondence with M. Knyazhevich and had ascertained that there
was a vacancy in the school for a Government scholar, and
they had got ready all the papers required for my applica-
tion. So, after a fortnight, when he had made acquaintance
through M. Knyazhevich with all the officials concerned,

my father, after fervent prayer to God, sent in his petition to M. Peken, the Rector of the school.

The governing body of the school appointed the Head Master, M. Kamashev, to examine me in my proficiency, and a Dr. Benis to conduct a medical examination. Kamashev was then on leave, and his duties were discharged in part by Vasili Upadishevsky, master of one of the dormitories; while the inspection of studies, of which Kamashev had charge, was carried on by Lyov Levitsky, the senior teacher of Russian Literature. Both these men proved kind and friendly, and Upadishevsky soon became a real guardian angel to me and to my mother; I do not know what would have become of us, but for this kind old friend. When my father went to the Rector's house to give in his petition, he took me with him, and the Rector proved very friendly. Next, as Levitsky was unwell and could not attend the meeting of the Governors, I was taken to his lodgings by my father. He too was very amiable and cheerful; he had a high color and, in spite of his youth, a considerable development behind his waistcoat. He charmed both of us by his reception. He began by kissing and embracing me. Then he set me something to read—prose by Karamzin and verse by Dmitriev—and was delighted to find that I read with intelligence and feeling. Next he made me write, and again my performance delighted him. In the four rules of arithmetic also I distinguished myself; but Levitsky, in the true spirit of a teacher of literature, expressed straight off his contempt for mathematics.

When the examination was over, he praised me without stint and expressed surprise that a boy of my age, living in the country, could be so well prepared. "Now who, pray, taught him to write?" he asked my father with a good-

humored laugh. "Your own handwriting is hardly a model."
My father, charmed and moved almost to tears by hearing his son praised, replied in the fullness of his heart that
I owed it all to my own hard work, under the supervision
of my mother, from whom I was almost inseparable, and
that he himself had taught me nothing but arithmetic. He
added that we had only lately moved to the country, that my
mother was a great lover of books and poetry and had spent
all her youth in a provincial capital, where her father held
an important position. "Ah," exclaimed Levitsky, "now I
understand the stamp of refinement, even of elegance, which
marks your charming boy; it is the fruit of a woman's work
of education, the result of a cultivated mother's labors." We
left the house enchanted with him.

Dr. Benis, who owned a fine house in Lyadsky Street,
received us very politely and made no difficulty about giving me a certificate of health and bodily vigor. On returning
home, I noticed that my mother had been weeping, though
her eyes had this peculiarity that tears did not cloud their
brightness and left no trace behind them. My father eagerly
reported all that had happened to us. My mother looked
at me with an expression that I shall never forget, even if I
have still a hundred years to live. She took me in her arms
and said, "You are my happiness, you are my pride!" What
more could I ask? In my own way, I was proud and happy,
too, and took courage.

My mother called on the wife of Dr. Benis and made
the acquaintance of the doctor himself. It was hard to deny
sympathy to my mother's youth and beauty, her intelligence
and her tears. They both quite fell in love with her, and the
doctor promised her that in any illness, however trifling, I
should enjoy all the resources of the medical art—a danger-

ous promise, according to my present ideas, when I dread an excess of medical attention; but it served then to comfort my poor mother to some extent.

Vasili Upadishevsky was a widower, and two of his own sons were Government scholars. My father made his acquaintance and invited him to visit us at our lodgings. My mother received him so kindly that he took a great fancy to her and was able to appreciate her maternal devotion. At their very first interview he promised her two things: to transfer me within a week to his own dormitory—to have done this at once for a new boy would have been thought a clear case of favoritism—and to look after me more closely than after his own "pair of scamps," by whom he meant his sons. Both promises were scrupulously fulfilled. I seem to see him now, with his kind courteous face and his right arm slung in a broad black ribbon; the hand had been blown off by the bursting of a cannon, and he wore a black glove stuffed with cotton-wool attached to the arm. He could write, however, very well and distinctly with his left hand.

At last all the formalities were complete, and the Governors decided to admit me to the school as a Government scholar. I was measured for my uniform, and the uniform was made. The strain which my mother and I were feeling did not grow less. We drove to the Cathedral and offered prayers to the three wonder-working saints of Kazan—Guri, Varsonofi, and Herman—and I was taken straight from the Cathedral to the school, and given over by my parents into the personal charge of Upadishevsky. My attendant, Yefrem Yevseich, came with me, taking service in the school as a dormitory man. The parting was, as may be supposed, accompanied by tears and blessings and good advice, but nothing remarkable took place. I was taken to the school at ten in the morning, when second lesson had just begun and all the boys were in the classrooms upstairs.* The bedrooms downstairs were empty, and my mother was able to examine them and to see the very bed in which I was to sleep; she seemed satisfied with all the arrangements. As soon as my parents had gone, Upadishevsky took my hand and led me to the writing class, where he introduced me to the teacher as a very well-disposed boy and begged him to pay special attention to me. I was put down with other new boys at a separate desk, and we were made to copy pot-hooks and hangers. I was quite dumbfounded and felt as if it was all a dream, but I had no sensation of fear or grief. After dinner, of which I remember nothing, I was made to put on a uniform jacket, with a cloth stock round my neck, and my hair was cut close. Then we were placed on parade in a line two deep—the boy next to me was Vladimir Graff—and we were taught at once how to march. I went mechanically through it all, as if I had nothing to do with it personally. When lessons were over, Upadishevsky met me at the door and said, "Your mother is waiting for you." Then he took me to the reception room where both my parents were standing.

When my father saw me, he laughed and said, "Well, one would hardly know Seryozha again!" But my mother, who had failed to recognize me at the first moment, threw up her hands, cried out, and fell fainting to the floor. I cried out wildly and fell at her feet. Upadishevsky, who had been looking through the chink of the door, was alarmed and

* In winter, first lesson began at 8 o'clock and second lesson at 10; work ended at noon and dinner came half an hour later. In summer, work began at 7 and ended at 11, and dinner was at noon exactly. At all seasons, afternoon school began at 2 and ended at 6, supper was at 8, and we went to bed at 9. We rose at 5 in the summer and 6 in the winter. (Author's note)

hurried to our aid. My mother's swoon, which lasted about half an hour, terrified my father and had such an effect upon poor Upadishevsky that he summoned from the hospital Ritter, the doctor's assistant, who gave some medicine to my mother and made me swallow something too. When my mother came to herself, she was very weak, and the kind-hearted Upadishevsky volunteered to give me leave to go home for the night. "M. Kamashev," said he, "may be angry with me, when he comes back and hears of it; and he would never have given leave himself. But never mind—I will take all the responsibility. Only please bring him back tomorrow at seven, just before the breakfast." We could not find words to thank him for such kindness, and off we went to our lodgings. At home my mother, on reflection, plucked up courage herself and breathed courage into me. She forced herself to look calmly at my close-cropped head, where her hand sought in vain the soft fair curls, and at the stock, which had already begun to rub the tender skin of my neck, unused even to a silk handkerchief. For everything she found a good reason which we had to submit to. Our mutual firmness and determination took hold of us with fresh power. I was at school the next day before seven o'clock. My mother paid me two visits every day, before dinner at midday, and again at six; the morning visit lasted only half an hour, but I could stay with her in the evening for an hour and a half. While we were together, she seemed peaceful and even happy, but I guessed from my father's sad face that matters were very different in my absence.

Within a few days, my father became convinced that things could not go on as they were, and that these constant meetings and partings were only a source of useless suffering. He took counsel with M. Knyazhevich, and the two decided that my mother should be taken back to the country without delay. It was easy to decide, but hard to carry out the decision, and this my father knew very well; but, much to his satisfaction and contrary to his expectation, my mother soon yielded to the entreaties and arguments addressed to her. Dr. Benis took an interest in the matter, and his words were undoubtedly of great weight. He assured her that these constant interviews were a trial to my nerves and dangerous to my health, and that, unless she went away, it would take me a long time to get accustomed to my new life, and perhaps I never should settle down at all. Even the soft-hearted Upadishevsky urged the same course; when he declared that I could not work properly in such a condition of affairs, and that my teachers would form a bad opinion of me, my mother consented to go away on the very next day. But there is one thing that still puzzles me: How she could make up her mind to play a trick on me. Before dinner she told me that she would leave the next day or the day after, and that we should meet twice more; she said too that she was spending that evening with the Knyazheviches, and would not visit me. To depart secretly and without saying good-bye—that was an unlucky idea, urged by Benis and Upadishevsky. Of course, they wished to spare us both, and me especially, the pain of a final parting, but their calculation was not verified. Even now I am convinced that this well-meant deception had many sad results.

It was the first time that my mother had omitted her evening visit, and though she had forewarned me, yet my heart ached with grief and a presentiment of some unknown calamity. I slept badly that night. Early next morning, when I began to dress, Yevseich handed me a note; it was my mother's farewell to me. She wrote that, if I loved her and desired her life and happiness, I must not grieve, but work hard at my lessons; she had left the town at eight on the previous evening. I remember that moment clearly, but I cannot describe it: A feeling of pain pierced my heart and compressed it, and stopped my breathing, and this was immediately followed by severe palpitation. I sat down on the bed half-dressed and looked round the room, dazed and despairing. Upadishevsky, who had moved me into his dormitory two days before, knew of my mother's departure and consequently understood the cause of my condition. Ordering that no one should touch me, he took all the other boys upstairs at once, handed them over to one of the masters, and hurried back to me. He found me sitting on my bed in the same position, and Yevseich in tears standing beside me. To all that he could say I turned a deaf ear. I could not form a single thought, and my eyes, as I was told afterwards, stared wildly. I was taken to the hospital; there too I sat down mechanically on a bed, and stared in silence as before. Within an hour Dr. Benis came. He examined me, shook his head, and said something in French; I heard later from others that the words were "pauvre enfant." I was given some repulsive medicine to swallow, undressed, and put to bed, where I was rubbed with flannel, and soon a violent fit of shivering restored me to consciousness. I called out loudly, "Mother has gone away!" and the streams of pent-up tears gushed from my eyes. This evidently relieved the doctor: He sat down beside me and began to speak of my mother's departure and of its necessity for the sake of her health, of the danger of a final interview, and of the way in which a sensible boy should behave in such a case, if he loved his mother and wished to set her mind at rest. His words were a real inspiration from above, for the doctor, though a very worthy man, was not exactly remarkable for gentleness of disposition. Though my tears flowed still faster, yet I felt better. The doctor left, and I sobbed on for two hours till

I cried myself to sleep; and kindly sleep did something to restore my strength. Upadishevsky came to see me several times and brought a book for me to read, *The Child's Instructor*, which I had never seen; he knew my passion for reading, but I was in no mood for it then. I asked leave to write, and wrote to my father and mother all that day and all the evening, crying most of the time. Yevseich never left me. Next morning the doctor found me in better health and discharged me from the hospital, thinking the society of invalids and the inactivity bad for me, but he directed that I should not be worked hard.

Upadishevsky himself took me back into school, where I found a writing-class going on; this was followed by a divinity lesson with the priest. For two hours I listened while the other boys repeated their lessons on the Catechism and Bible history and the priest set a fresh lesson and explained some difficulty at great length, but I could not understand his explanations either on this occasion or on any other while I remained at the school. I had not learned the lesson for that day, and the priest had been informed of my illness; a strict and severe man, he did not go beyond a reprimand, but told me to have my lesson prepared next time. After dinner, in order that I might not remain idle and a prey to sad thoughts, Upadishevsky handed me over to one of the older boys who drew well, Ilya Zhevanov, that he might amuse me in that way; as a child I had had a great fancy for drawing. I myself heard the kind old man say to Zhevanov, "Please do me a great kindness which I shall never forget, and amuse this poor homesick boy by drawing with him," and Zhevanov consented. But neither then nor later did my drawing come to anything: the copying of circles, eyebrows, noses, eyes, and lips, had set me against drawing for good and all.

At the end of afternoon school, Upadishevsky, still my good genius, made me repeat my lessons beside him; and when he saw that I did not understand what I was saying, he began to talk to me of my life at home and of my parents, and even allowed me to cry a little. I do not know how life would have gone on with me, but at this point there came a complete and sudden change. The next day but one, during dinner, Yevseich handed me a note from my mother, which said that, after traveling ninety versts from Kazan, she had come back to have at least a momentary glimpse of me; to leave without a proper parting had proved too much for her. I cannot explain to myself why I did not at the first moment feel the immense happiness that I surely ought to have felt. I suppose I was afraid to believe it and took it for a dream. There was a note also for Upadishevsky: my mother asked him to give me leave from six till nine in the evening, or if that was impossible, she would come herself; she added that she would spend only one night in Kazan. He told me to write to my mother that she was not to be anxious and not to come herself; he would send me with Yevseich, perhaps before six, as the teacher of the last lesson was not well and would probably not turn up; and I might stay with her till seven next morning. As I wrote all this, I felt sure that I was in a dream. Yevseich hastened off with my letter and returned in an hour and a half with an answer of such joy and gratitude to Upadishevsky that the old man's eyes grew wet as he read it. Yevseich told us that his mistress had returned alone; she had turned back at a village ninety versts away along the post road; his master had remained there with the young lady, who was not well; and my mother had traveled with post-horses in a light courier's sledge, accompanied by one maid and one man. I began to realize the situation and to believe in my good fortune, and was soon so completely convinced of it that the last hour of suspense was a terrible trial. The teacher sent notice that he would not come, and at five minutes past four I got into a hired sledge, attended by Yevseich and crazy with happiness beyond description.

My mother was staying with some friends whose name I forget; but it was certainly not at an inn. When I ran into the room, I saw her, looking pale and thin, wrapped up in a warm cloak, and sitting beside a newly lighted stove, as the room was very cold. The first moment of our meeting it is impossible for me to describe; but never again in my life did I experience a thrill of happiness to compare with that. For some minutes we were silent and only wept for joy. But this did not last long: the thought of coming separation soon drove all other thoughts and feelings from me, and made my heart ache. With bitter tears I told my mother all that had happened to me since her sudden departure. I was frightened by the effect of my story. How my poor mother blamed herself, and repented of her promise to deceive me and go away without saying good-bye! Then she told me about herself. She had fainted on getting into the sledge, and had no recollection of leaving Kazan. As she got farther away, her suffering increased every hour, and soon the idea of returning took hold of her; but my father's arguments and her own good sense restrained her for some time from the course on which her heart was set. At last she was unable any longer to withstand her feelings, and she returned alone; my sister, unwell already and unfit for travel, needed rest and was to wait with my father till my mother rejoined them. That whole evening, and most of the night, was spent by us in talking and in weeping; but, as there are limits to all things, we came to an end of our tears and went to sleep. I remember how I started in my sleep several times and began sobbing, till my mother took me in her arms and laid my head on her breast, and I fell asleep again. We were wakened at six o'clock. We were calmer and braver by that time. My mother promised that, as soon as the roads were open in summer,* she would come to Kazan and stay till the examinations were over, and after the Speech Day, which was always near the beginning of July, she would take me home for the holidays which would last till the middle of August. A feeling of comfort filled my heart, and we said good-bye calmly enough. At seven my mother got into the sledge she had come in, and Yevseich and I into another, and we all started together. She drove to the right, towards the town gate, and I to the left, towards the school; we soon turned off the main street, and her sledge vanished from my sight.

My heart ached, and a load of pain lay on my breast, but my head was perfectly clear, and I fully understood all that was going on around me and all that lay ahead of me in the future. The great white building of the school, with its bright green roof and cupola, stood on a hill, and the sudden appearance of it surprised me as much as if I had never seen it before. It seemed to me like a terrible enchanted castle such as I had read of, or a prison where I was to be shut up as a convict. The great door between columns at the top of a flight of steps, which, when it was opened by the old pensioner, I felt had swallowed me up, the two broad high staircases, lit from the cupola and leading from the hall to the first and second floors, the shouting and confused noise of many voices that came from all the classrooms to meet me, the teachers being still absent—all this I saw and heard and understood for the first time. I had already spent more

---

* The spring thaw made traveling impossible for a time.

than a week in the school but had never realized it; now for
the first time I felt myself to be a Government scholar in a
Government school.

The whole day each thing that happened was new and
surprising, and oh! how repulsive it all seemed to me! We
rose at the sound of a bell, long before daylight, when there
was an intolerable smell in the rooms from the guttering
or extinguished night-lights and tallow candles; the cold
in the dormitories made rising even more unpleasant for
a poor child who could barely keep warm under his frieze
coverlet;* we washed all together at copper basins, which
were always the scene of quarrels and fights; we marched
two and two to prayers, to breakfast, to lessons, to dinner,
and to everything; our breakfast consisted of a roll and a
glass of milk and water in equal proportions, with a glass
of *sbiten*† instead of milk and water on fast days; we had
three courses at dinner and two at supper, but they were
not better meals than breakfast. How was all this likely to
strike a boy whom his mother had petted and made much
of and brought up as luxuriously as if we had been very
rich? But more terrible to me than anything else were my
companions. The oldest boys and those in the middle of the
school took no notice of me, but those of my own age or
even younger, who were at the bottom of the school, were
for the most part intolerably rude and rough. Though there
were exceptions, I had so little in common even with them,
and we differed so much in ideas and interests and habits,
that I could not make friends with them, and I remained

---

* The temperature of the dormitories was kept at 53°, as is still the custom in all Government schools. In my opinion, this is positively harmful
to children; it ought not to be lower than 58°. (Author's note)

† A drink made of honey and hot water.

solitary in the midst of numbers. They were all healthy and contented and unbearably cheerful, and not a single one of them was in the least degree depressed or thoughtful or likely to sympathize with my constant sadness. If there had been, I would have rushed boldly into his arms and shared my secret with him. "How strange it is!" I said to myself. "These boys cannot have father or mother, brothers or sisters, nor house and garden in the country," and I was inclined to pity them. But I soon found out that almost all of them had parents and families, and some even had homes in the country with gardens; but one thing they had not—that feeling of intense attachment to home and family that filled my own heart. As a matter of course, I at once became an object of ridicule to my companions: I was a nincompoop, a crybaby, and a milksop who was always "blubbering for his mama." Upadishevsky never ceased to watch over me night and day, but neither his authority nor his moral influence could shield me from this form of persecution. He told me himself never to complain of the boys' mockery, as he knew very well how "sneaks" are hated in schools, and that this label is attached to any persecuted boy who ventures to complain to the authorities. He put my bed between the beds of two much older boys; their names were Kondiryov and Moreyev; both were well-behaved boys and also hard workers. He handed me over to their protection, and thanks to them, no young scamp ventured to approach my bed. I should mention that in those days our accommodation was so limited that the Government scholars and pensioners* spent all the time that they were not in school in their dormitories.

* Boys who paid for their education and maintenance.

After finally parting from my mother, I began at once to work hard at my lessons. Through Upadishevsky I asked my teachers to set me twice or thrice as much as the usual tasks, in order to catch up to the older boys and get promotion from the newcomers' bench. My memory and power of understanding were already strongly developed, and within a month I had not only distanced my contemporaries, but was placed on the top bench in all subjects, side by side with the best scholars. This circumstance made me even more unpopular with both those whom I had passed and those who were still my rivals.

Just at this time the Head Master, Nikolai Kamashev, returned to his duties. He was considered a very able man. I do not know if he deserved this reputation, but he certainly was a cold, hard man, who always spoke low and with a smile, but always acted with inflexible determination. Without exception, everyone feared him much more than they did the Rector. He loved power, knew how to acquire it, and was exacting to pedantry in his use of it. Upadishevsky had foreseen that he would get into trouble; in fact, Kamashev at once discovered all the departures from school rules that had been sanctioned by his representative for my mother and me—interviews with parents at times not recognized by the rules, unlawful leave home, and (worst of all) leave for the night. My benefactor got such a reprimand that the old gentleman walked about for a long time looking very serious. Kamashev had said to him with his quiet smile, "If anything of the kind ever occurs in future, I shall request you, my dear Sir, to retire from your service in this school." When I heard of this, I shed bitter tears and conceived an invincible aversion and horror for the very name of the Head Master. And I had some reason, for he took a dislike to me without cause and became my persecutor, and his oppression cost my poor mother many tears in the end.

Three days after his return, Kamashev summoned me out of the ranks to the center of the hall and delivered for my benefit a rather long address: A spoiled boy, he said, was a regular nuisance, and it was mean to take advantage of undue indulgence shown by authorities, and wrong to be ungrateful to the Government which generously took upon itself the considerable expense of my education. Though mild and quiet by disposition, I was naturally sensitive and excitable. I stood there, with my eyes on the floor, while a feeling hitherto unknown swelled within my breast, a feeling of anger at undeserved insult. "Why do you not look at me?" Kamashev called out. "It is a bad sign, when a boy hides his eyes and dares not, or will not, look his master in the face." Then he raised his voice and said in a severe tone, "Look at me!" I raised my eyes, and I suppose they expressed pretty clearly the feeling of insulted pride that filled my young breast, for he turned away and said, as he went out, to Upadishevsky, "That boy is by no means as mild and good-tempered as you make out." I heard afterwards that he wished to remove me from the dormitory I was in, and demanded reports from all my teachers and masters; but when he found in all of them "Conduct and diligence exemplary, proficiency remarkable," he left me where I was. During the whole of my first term, he constantly examined my books and notebooks in form and made the teachers question me in his presence; sometimes he found fault with me for trifles or told the masters that they must make me play with the other boys, adding, "I don't like your silent solitary boys."

I understand now that such a criticism is justified in some cases, but it was quite unsuitable to mine and only increased my natural irritation. Upadishevsky really loved me and watched over me with a mother's care; every day he inspected my clothes and bedding, and saw that my hands were clean and my books in good order. He often impressed upon me that I must look the Head Master straight in the face and bear his remarks and reprimands in silence, and I carried out these instructions exactly, because I loved Upadishevsky.

But this did not conciliate Kamashev. By the school rules, none of the boys might have private property or money of their own; if they had money, it was kept by the dormitory master and might not be spent without the Head Master's consent. To buy food or sweets was strictly forbidden. Of course, there were breaches of this rule, but they were carefully concealed. There was also a rule that boys' letters to their parents and relations should pass through the hands of the masters; each boy was obliged to give his letter, before it was sealed and sent to the post, to the dormitory master, who had a right to read it if he felt any distrust of the writer. Though this rule was in practice disregarded, Kamashev instructed Upadishevsky to show him my letters. The kind old man had always added a postscript to my letters home without reading them; now he was obliged to harden his heart and act as censor of what I wrote. My first letter that he read placed him in a very difficult position: I described the grief I suffered daily, I complained of my companions and even of my teachers, and I expressed a burning desire to see my mother and to leave the hateful school as soon as possible and spend the summer in the country; and that was all. There was nothing wrong in it, but the reader felt sure that every word would be criminal in the eyes of the Head Master, that he would find there discontent, criticism of authority, calumny against the school, and ingratitude to the Government. What was to be done? Upadishevsky was unwilling at once to reveal to me the actual state of affairs, for that would be much the same as conspiring with a boy against his superior. He felt also that I would not understand him, and would be unable to write a letter of the kind that Kamashev would approve; but to deprive my mother of my frank and full letters, which were her only consolation, was impossible to his kind heart. For a whole night and day he puzzled over the difficulty without finding a solution— he told me this himself afterwards—and at last made up his mind to tell me the whole truth and at the same time to play a trick upon his senior and superior. Accordingly, he dictated to me another letter in a purely formal style and showed this to Kamashev, who naturally could find nothing in it to blame me for. Both letters were sent together to the post. After this I wrote two letters every time, one for show and the other private, and I went on with this, even after my tyrant had ceased to read my correspondence. Upadishevsky himself wrote at once to my mother, to explain the reason for this contrivance. Yevseich took the letters to the post in person. I could not then appreciate the full extent of my benefactor's self-sacrifice, but my mother could, and she wrote to Upadishevsky and expressed the most ardent gratitude that a mother's heart could feel. I need hardly say that, though she did not know all the details of it, she was much agitated by Kamashev's persecution of her son.

Things continued to go on as before, but a change took place in me which ought to have seemed strange and unnatural to those around me. For though in the course of six weeks I ought to have become accustomed to the new life, I became thoughtful and sad; and then sadness led to fits of misery and finally to illness. The change was probably due to two causes. When I had caught up to my classmates in all our lessons, I was given ordinary tasks which were so short that I often learned them before we were let out of school, and consequently had nothing to do in our free time; and my active mind, deprived of proper nourishment, turned exclusively in one direction. I was constantly turning over and considering my present situation, constantly picturing all that was going on at home, dwelling on my mother's longing for me, and recalling the old days of bliss spent in the country. In my heart I hated the school and was convinced in my own mind that the process of education was entirely useless and only served to turn innocent children into objectionable boys. The second and perhaps the main cause of the change was the unfair persecution by Kamashev. Each time he appeared, he gave a shock to my nerves, and he paid two visits every day at unfixed times. There was no hour, day or night, at which he might not make a perfectly sudden and unexpected appearance in the school. I am able now to do justice to his ceaseless activity, though it was too strict and mechanical; but then he seemed to me a mere tyrant, an ogre, an evil spirit, who appeared to spring out of the earth even in places that were safe from the eye of the other masters. His terrible image haunted my young brain, and the oppression of his presence was always with me. In the meantime, my secret letters to my mother became much shorter than before, and I wrote them with ever-increasing anxiety and caution. For I now understood the constraint that Upadishevsky was putting upon his honest and open nature, and the risk he ran. A third reason for the change in me was produced by the course of time. By the end of March and beginning of April the sun became very hot, the snow melted, the streams of water flowed through the streets; there was a breath of spring in the air, and this was a trial to the nerves of a child who had a passionate, if still unconscious, love of nature. It is a known fact that the sun's rays in spring have a disturbing effect on the constitution, and I distinctly remember that I was much more depressed on sunny days than when the weather was dull.

Be that as it may, I became "absorbed." I mean that I ceased to listen to the talk of others: I learned my lessons and repeated them without interest; I heard the criticism or approval of my teachers, but all the time, while I was looking them straight in the face, I was fancying myself at dear Aksakovo, sheltered by my mother's love in my peaceful home. This always passed for mere inattention. To give greater reality to my dreams, which grew more vivid every day, I used to shut my eyes, and was often jogged by my neighbors who thought I was sleeping. One day, during a lesson in Russian Grammar, a malicious boy named Rushka called out, "Aksakov is asleep!" The teacher asked other boys whether this was true, and nearly punished me by making me kneel down, when they said that it was. I did not shut my eyes in school after that; but when I had said my lesson, I often made use of a familiar pretext to leave the room; and then I could sometimes stand in peace for a quarter of an hour in some passage corner, and close my eyes, and dream. When afternoon school was over, the boys ran about for half an hour in the reception hall, while I kept out of it, if I was allowed. Then we had all to sit down, each at the little table by his bed, and learn the lessons for next day. I too sat down and placed a book before me, and amid the murmur of boys' voices conning over their lessons, my thoughts always traveled to the same spot, the paradise of my country home on the bank of the Buguruslan.

Soon, however, this violent strain upon the imagination reached a pitch that proved injurious to my health. I began to suffer from hysterical fits, accompanied by such violent

weeping and sobbing that I lost consciousness for some minutes; I was told later that at such times the muscles of my
face were convulsed. I was able at first to conceal my condition to some extent from observation. I did this uncon-
sciously; perhaps a secret feeling told me that I should be
prevented from giving myself up to those dreams, which
were my only comfort. The trouble generally came upon
me in the evening; I felt it coming, and used to run down
the back stairs to an inner yard, where all the boys might
go in case of necessity; or sometimes I hid behind a pillar, sometimes in the corner formed by the high staircase
where it rose from the center of the building; sometimes I
ran upstairs and sat in a corner of the landing on the first
floor, which was dimly lighted from below by a hanging
lamp. The cold air probably helped to shorten the attack,
and I could go back to my place in my usual condition. But
once, I took refuge in an open classroom that was being
cleaned out, and hid, though I cannot remember doing this,
under one of the desks. I fancy that this fit lasted unusually
long, and perhaps this was due to the close atmosphere of
the room where it came on. A porter noticed me and tried
to turn me out, but when I did not answer him, he told a
tutor, who recognized me and informed Upadishevsky. The
old man ran upstairs in great alarm, but it happened that I
recovered at that very moment and went quietly with him
back to the dormitory.

Before this incident Upadishevsky had felt fairly easy
about me. I had been nearly two months in the school
and was showing diligence in my studies; and, though
he noticed that I was often either inattentive or absorbed
in some way, he attached no special importance to this.
Now he questioned me minutely, and I told him fully and
frankly all I knew of my own condition, but there was much

I could not understand and much I could not remember. Throughout the night, he and Yevseich watched over me, and I slept quite peacefully till morning. I ought to say that throughout the first period of my illness I always slept well at night; I mention this because in the later stages sleeplessness was one of the chief symptoms. Early next morning, Dr. Benis came as usual to the hospital, where I had been taken by Upadishevsky. He questioned me and examined me attentively, and found me rather thin and pale and my pulse irregular. Yet he prescribed no medicine and let me go back into school. I was not to work too hard—he did not believe me when I said my lessons were too easy— and he gave directions that I was to be watched and not allowed to go anywhere alone. He added that he wished to see me every morning at the time of his visit to the hospital. Upadishevsky took all necessary measures: he visited me constantly himself, and put me in the charge of two boys who were to keep an eye on me whenever we were out of school; and Yevseich was told to go with me, every time I went out to the back yard. A report spread throughout the school that I was catching the "black sickness,"* and I was frightened, though I did not understand the meaning of the words. It seemed to me very unpleasant that outsiders should keep constant watch over my every movement, and I felt listless and sad all that evening. The pleasure of my daydreams was now familiar, and the thought that I was being watched by several pairs of eyes prevented me from enjoying this pleasure and burying the bitter reality out of sight; but, for all that, the evening passed off successfully—I had no violent distress or hysterical attack. Upadishevsky and Yevseich were delighted; the doctor also was much pleased

* Epilepsy.

when I visited him next day in the hospital and he was told that I had spent the whole day and night in peace. Though he found my pulse as irregular as before, he gave me no medicine and let me go, declaring that things would come right and that nature would overcome unaided whatever was amiss.

But next day it turned out that the evil was not cured but only changed: at nine in the morning, during a lesson in arithmetic, I felt a sudden severe oppression on the chest, and a few minutes later burst out sobbing and then fell senseless on the floor. There was a great stir, and Upadishevsky was sent for. By good fortune, he was in the house,* and he had me carried to the dormitory, where I came to myself in a quarter of an hour, and even went back into school. But in the evening there was a second fit which lasted much longer. My kind benefactor and my devoted attendant were excessively alarmed. This time the doctor gave me some drops, which I was to take whenever I felt the oppression coming on; on fast days I was to have ordinary food from the hospital and a roll instead of brown bread; but on no account was he willing that I should stay in the hospital. The drops did me good at first, and I had no fainting-fit for three days, though I was depressed and cried at times, but then, whether it was that my system became accustomed to the medicine or that the illness was gaining strength, the fits grew more frequent and more violent.

No period of my childhood do I remember with more perfect distinctness than my first term at school. I could describe accurately and with every detail—though I cer-

* Of the four ushers, two were always on duty and on the spot; but the other two might absent themselves during school time; at dinner and supper all four were present. (Author's note)

tainly have no intention of doing so—the whole course of my strange malady. Like everyone else, I believed at the time that no cause could be assigned for the coming-on of these fits. Now I am convinced of the contrary: they were always produced by some sudden recollection of that past life, which presented itself to me in a moment, with all the liveliness and clearness of dreams at night. Sometimes I reached these manifestations consciously and gradually, by plunging into the inexhaustible treasury of recollection, but at other times they visited me without any wish or thought of mine. When I was thinking of something quite different, even when I was entirely taken up by my lessons, suddenly the sound of someone's voice, probably like some voice I had heard before, or a patch of sunlight on wall or window, such as had once before thrown light in just the same way upon objects dear and familiar, or a fly buzzing and beating against the panes, as I had often watched them do when I was a child—such sights and sounds, though no consciousness could detect the process, for one instant recalled the forgotten past and gave a shock to my overstrung nerves.

In some cases, however, the explanation was clear at once. Thus I was saying a lesson one day, when suddenly a pigeon perched on the windowsill and began to turn round and coo; at once I thought of my pet pigeons at home, and the oppression on my chest came on immediately and was followed by a fit. Another time I went for a drink of water or *kvass* to the room used for that purpose, and there I suddenly caught sight of a plain deal table that I had probably seen many times before without noticing it. But now it had been newly planed and looked notably clean and white, and instantly there flashed before me another wooden table which looked like that and was always perfectly white and smooth. It had belonged to my grandmother and afterwards stood in my aunt's room; and on it were kept various tri-fles, precious in a child's eyes—packets of melon seeds with which my aunt used to make wonderful little baskets and trays, little bags of carob beans and pebbles, and above all, a large needle book, which held not only needles but also fish-ing hooks which my grandmother dealt out to me from time to time. In former days I used to gaze at all these treasures with intense interest and breathless excitement. As soon as the likeness between the tables struck me, the past flashed into life and brightness before me, and the familiar sensa-tions of uneasiness were soon followed by a severe attack. The result was the same when I happened to see a sleeping cat curled up in the sun and was reminded of my own pet cat at home. These instances are, I think, sufficient to jus-tify the hypothesis of similar causes in the other cases of the kind.

My condition went from bad to worse. The fits became more frequent and lasted longer; I lost appetite and became paler and thinner daily, and I lost also my eagerness for study; I owed my remaining strength to sleep alone. As the watchful eye of Upadishevsky had noticed that early ris-ing was bad for me, one day he tried the experiment of not waking me till eight, and all that day I felt much better. Yev-seich waited on me with the tenderness of a father. Kama-shev tried another method: he lectured me severely more than once, and even threatened to punish me, if I did not behave as a well-conducted boy ought to do. My illness, he said, was only the fancifulness of a spoiled child, and a bad example to the rest. At last, he gave a positive order that I should be moved to the hospital. I wished this myself, and so did everyone else. Dr. Benis, who alone took the oppo-site view, was now obliged to give way, and I was removed to the sick room.

When my mother was leaving Kazan for the second time, she made Yevseich swear before a sacred picture that he would let her know if I fell ill. For a long time he had been burning to fulfill his promise, and spoke of it to Upadishevsky, but the master always kept him back. Now, however, he decided to act without consulting anyone, and got one of the servants, who had acquired the art, to write a letter in which, with no precautions and without due regard to the facts, he reported that his young master was suffering from epilepsy and had been taken to the hospital.

It is easy to imagine how this letter dropped like a thunderbolt upon my parents. The post was slow, and the letter reached them at the time of the spring thaw, when the roads are in a state quite inconceivable by people who live near Moscow. At every step, the traveler came on places where the road was washed away, and every hollow was filled by melting snowdrifts; for a carriage to pass was almost impossible. But nothing could keep my mother back; she started the same day for Kazan, attended by her devoted Parasha and Parasha's young husband, Theodore. She drove day and night in a rough, peasant sledge drawn by one horse without shoes;* they had three sledges, each holding one passenger, while a fourth was given up to the baggage; they had only such horses as the peasants could supply. This was the only way in which it was just possible to push on step by step; and even so, they had to take advantage of the morning frosts, which fortunately went on that year till the middle of April. Ten days of this traveling brought my mother to the large village of Murzikha on the bank of the Kama; the main road used by the post went this way, and

---

* At this season, when the snow is deep on the side roads, horses travel better unshod. (Author's note)

it was more possible to travel along it, as it was hardened by traffic. But, on the other hand, it was necessary to cross the Kama, in order to reach the village of Shuran, which is situated, I think, about eighty versts from Kazan. The river had not melted yet, but the ice was blue and swollen. The post had been carried across it the day before by runners on foot, but rain had fallen in the night, and the villagers all refused to convey my mother and her companions across to the other side. She was forced to spend the night in the village. Dreading every moment of delay, she walked herself from house to house, imploring kind people to help her, explaining her grief, and offering all she possessed to recompense them. And she did find kind and brave hearts, who understood a mother's sorrow; they promised that, if the rain stopped in the night and there was the least trace of frost in the morning, they would land her in safety on the farther bank, and would accept whatever she pleased to give them for their trouble.

The whole of that night my mother spent upon her knees before the sacred picture which hung in a corner of the hut where she lodged. Her fervent prayer was heard: a wind rose and dispersed the clouds, and by morning frost had dried the road and covered the pools with a thin coating of ice. At daybreak six stout fellows presented themselves, all fishermen by calling, born on the banks of the river and accustomed to deal with it in all its aspects; each was armed with a pole and carried a light burden bound on his back. Before starting, they crossed themselves, turning towards the cross on the church. They gave Theodore a pole and also a creel which he was to drag by a rope; the creel was a large basket with a projecting peak, and they took this in case the lady should be too weary to walk. Then they took by the hand the two women, who had put on men's long boots, and started, after sending ahead the most active of their mates to feel the way before them. The track over the ice was slanting, so that it was necessary to cover nearly three versts. To cross a great river on foot at that season is so dangerous that only an adept can perform the feat, using all his courage and presence of mind. Theodore and Parasha simply howled, and said good-bye to this world and all their nearest and dearest; and in some places force had to be used to compel them to go on, but my mother's courage and even cheerfulness increased with every step. Her guides kept wagging their heads in astonished admiration when they looked at her. They had to go round gaps in the ice and to cross a crevasse on the poles laid side by side. My mother for long refused to make use of the creel, but when they were approaching the opposite side, and the track led over shallows close to the bank, and all danger was past, then she felt her strength leave her. Pillows and a fur-lined coverlet were at once placed on the creel, and my mother lay down upon it and nearly fainted on the spot; in this condition the fishermen dragged her as far as the post house of Shuran. She gave her guides a hundred rubles, just half the money she had upon her, but the honest fishermen would not take it, and asked five rubles apiece. They listened with wonder to the thanks and blessings which my mother showered down upon them, and they said at parting, "God bring you safe to the end of your journey!" Then they started at once on their homeward way; there was need for haste, for the ice broke up the next day. All these details I heard later from Parasha. My mother traveled from Shuran to Kazan in forty-eight hours; she stopped at the first inn she came to, and she was in the school building an hour later.

And now I go back to myself. I was very comfortably installed in the hospital, in a small room by myself; it was intended for severe cases, but there happened to be none at the time. Yevseich was transferred to the hospital to work there, and slept in my room. Andrei Ritter—a surgeon or assistant-surgeon, I am not sure which—had a room near me. He was a handsome lively fellow, tall and ruddy. He was at home only in the mornings until Dr. Benis came, and then went off immediately to visit his patients—for he actually had some practice among the merchant class; he was very dissipated and often returned home late at night and far from sober. I wonder that the Head Master tolerated him; he paid more attention, however, to the sound than to the sick, and Upadishevsky had greater influence in the hospital. I have entirely forgotten the name and surname of the good-natured old man who was then in charge of the place, though I have a clear recollection of his kindness to me. Upadishevsky took care that time should not hang heavy on my hands and at once provided me with books—*The Child's Instructor* in several volumes, *The Discovery of America*, and *The Conquest of Mexico*. How delighted I was with the quiet and peace and books to read! A dressing gown instead of my uniform, perfect freedom in the disposal of my time, no bell to listen for, and books to read—all this did me more good than any medicine or nourishing diet. Columbus and Pizarro aroused all my interest, and the hapless Montezuma all my sympathy. In a few days I had finished *The Discovery of America* and *The Conquest of Mexico*, and then set to work on *The Child's Instructor*.

While I was reading this I came across something that puzzled me very much; indeed, I was much older before I found a complete solution of the difficulty. In one of the volumes I found a fairy tale called *Beauty and the Beast*. The first lines seemed to me familiar, and the further I read, the more familiar it became, till at last I felt certain that this was the story which I knew by the title of *The Scarlet Flower** and had heard a score of times from our housekeeper Pelageya.

This Pelageya was a remarkable woman in her way. While very young, she had run away with her father from her owners, the Alakayevs, to Astrakhan, where she lived more than twenty years. Her father soon died; she married, and lost her husband, and then went out to service in merchants' families. Growing tired of this, she somehow learned that she had become the property of a different owner—my grandfather, in fact—a strict master but just and kind-hearted; and, a year before his death, the truant turned up at Aksakovo. My grandfather respected her for coming back without compulsion and received her kindly; and soon, as she was a notable woman and could turn her hand to anything, he took a great fancy to her and made her his housekeeper, a kind of post which she had held before at Astrakhan. Apart from her skill in household management, Pelageya brought with her a remarkable gift for telling fairy tales, of which she knew an immense number. It is obvious that the natives of the East have imparted to the Russians at Astrakhan a strong taste for hearing and telling these stories. In the comprehensive repertoire of Pelageya, there were not only Russian stories but a number of Eastern tales, including some from *The Arabian Nights*. My grandfather was delighted to possess such a treasure, and as he was beginning to fail in health and slept badly, Pelageya, who could boast of another valuable quality, the power of staying awake all night, did much to ease the old man's suffering. From her I too heard no end of fairy tales in the long winter evenings. The image of Pelageya, with

* This story is given in full in an appendix to the author's *Years of Childhood*.

her fresh, healthy face and stout figure, and with the spindle
and distaff in her hands, is ineffaceably engraved upon my
memory; if I were an artist, I could paint her to the life this
very minute. The story of *Beauty and the Beast* or *The Scarlet
Flower* was to surprise me once again some years later, when
I went to the theater at Kazan to see an opera called *Zemira
and Azor*, and found it was *The Scarlet Flower* over again, both
in the general story and in the details.

Meantime, in spite of interesting books and delightful
confabulations with Yevseich about life at home with its
fishing and hawks and pigeons; in spite of removal from
school with its tiresome noise and troublesome companions;
in spite of the quantity of pills and powders and mixtures
I swallowed down—my illness, which seemed at first to be
yielding to treatment and rest, did not grow less, and the
fits recurred several times a day. For some reason, however, they did not frighten me, and when I compared it with
the past, I was quite content with my condition. The hospital was on the second story, with windows looking on the
court. The school building, now the University, stood on a
hill and commanded a fine view: all the lower half of the city
with its suburbs, and the great lake of Kaban, whose waters
mingle in spring with the overflow of the Volga—this was
the picturesque panorama that spread out before my eyes.
I remember clearly how the darkness settled down upon it,
and how the morning dawn and the sunrise used little by
little to light it up. In general, my stay in the hospital has
left on my mind a lasting recollection of peace and consolation, though none of my schoolfellows ever visited me. The
Knyazhevich boys came only once; I was not very intimate
with them then because we did not meet much: they were
halfway up the school and lived in the "French dormitory,"
where Meissner was tutor. Besides, I was so much taken up

with myself, or rather with my past life, that I never showed or felt the least attachment for them. But we became close friends in my second term at school and, still more, in our college days.

I wrote home by every post and always said that I was quite well. But a Monday came without bringing me a letter from my mother. I felt anxious and sad, and when there was no letter on the following Monday, I was miserable. Yevseich tried to reassure me: he said that owing to the season and state of the roads it was impossible to send a carriage from Aksakovo to Buguruslan—our country town, twenty-five versts distant from our house. But I would not listen to him. I knew perfectly that in all weathers they sent once a week to the post without fail. I don't know what I should have done if my letter had failed me a third time. But in the middle of the week—the exact date 18 of April, in the morn-ing—my kind Yevseich began in a roundabout way to this effect, that the absence of letters might be accounted for by a visit from my mother herself, and that perhaps she had actu-ally arrived. After this preparation, he announced with a beaming face that Sofya Nikolaevna was now in the school and that, though she might not visit me in the absence of the doctor, the doctor was coming at once. Though I had been prepared for this news, I fainted away. When I recovered, my first words were, "Where is Mama?" But Dr. Benis was standing by me and scolding Yevseich. He was not in the least to blame; however cautiously I had been told of my mother's arrival, I could not have received such joyful and unexpected tidings without strong emotion, and any emo-tion would have brought on a seizure. The doctor was quite convinced that permission must be given for the mother to see her son, especially when the son knew of her arrival; but he did not venture to give it without being authorized by the Head Master or Rector, and he had sent notes to them both. The Rector's permission came first, and my mother was actually in my room, when an order came from Kamashev to await his arrival.

For want of words, I shall not attempt to describe what I felt when my mother came into the room. She was so thin that I might not have known her, but her joy at finding her child not only alive but much better than she expected—what did not her anxious heart forebode?—shone so radiantly in her eyes, which were always bright, that an onlooker might have supposed her both well and cheerful. All my surroundings were forgotten; I clasped her in my arms and for some time would not let her go. A few minutes later Kamashev appeared. With cold politeness he told my mother that the regular rules of the school had been broken on her account—that relations or parents were not permitted to enter the inner rooms of the establishment, but only the reception room specially provided for the purpose, and that admission to the hospital was absolutely forbidden, and especially undesirable in the case of a lady so young and so attractive.

The blood rushed to my mother's face; she was naturally impulsive, and she now told Kamashev more home truths than were necessary. Among other things she said, "Your school must be the only school in the world that has such a barbarous rule! A mother's presence is desirable in any place where her son is lying ill! I am here by permission of the Rector, your immediate superior, Mr. Head Master, and all you have to do is to obey!" She had plunged her knife into the tender spot. Kamashev turned pale. He then said, "The Rector has given leave for once only, and his order has been obeyed; it will probably not be repeated, and I beg that you will now go away." But he did not know my mother, nor did he understand the feelings common to all mothers' hearts. She told him that she would not leave that room till the Rector, either in person or by letter, ordered her to go; until that happened nothing short of actual violence should part her from her son. And this was said with such vehemence and in such a tone that it was quite certain she would carry it out to the letter. She took a chair, pushed it up to my bed, and sat down on it with her back turned to Kamashev. What he would have done I do not know, had not Dr. Benis and Upadishevsky induced him to go to another room, where, as I heard later from Upadishevsky, the doctor spoke firmly to him.

"If," said he, "you venture on any violent measures, I will not be responsible for the consequences; it may even kill the boy, and I am anxious about the mother too." Upadishevsky also implored him to be merciful to a poor woman who was in such despair that she did not know what she was saying, and still more to have pity on a poor sick boy; and he promised that he would persuade my mother to go away before long. Kamashev gave way very reluctantly, and went off with the doctor to report the whole affair to the Rector. Upadishevsky went back to my mother and tried to quiet her by saying that she might stay with me two hours. She did stay till dark, till nearly six in the evening. The scene with Kamashev frightened me at first, and I was beginning to feel the familiar pressure on the chest, but when he left the room, the fit was stopped by my mother's presence, her conversation and caresses, and my own happiness. At parting, my mother said positively that she would remove me from the school altogether and take me back home, and I believed her implicitly. I was accustomed to think that she could do whatever she liked, and a bright future began to shine before me in all the rainbow colors of the happy past.

On leaving the school, my mother went straight to Dr. Benis's house. He was not at home, and she threw herself, literally threw herself, at the feet of his wife and implored her with tears to help in rescuing her son from the school. Mme. Benis understood a mother's feeling and was keenly interested. She said that her husband would do what he could, and she would vouch for his assistance. The doctor soon came in, and both ladies, each in her own way, pressed him hard. But he needed no convincing. He said that he quite agreed and had hinted at this course to the Rector; unfortunately, the Head Master was there too, and his strong opposition to the plan had apparently prevailed with the Rector, a weak but not ill-natured man; nevertheless, success was not beyond hope. Next, my mother described all the unfairness and petty tyranny which I had suffered from the Head Master. As Benis himself disliked the man for his usurpation of power that did not belong to him, he served to increase rather than allay my mother's exasperation till she positively hated Kamashev as the cruelest of enemies to herself and her son. The doctor and his wife treated her with the kindness of friends or relations. They made her lie down on a sofa and take some food, twenty-four hours having passed since she had tasted even tea; they gave her some medicine, and above all, they assured her that my illness was purely nervous and that I should soon get perfectly well in my country home. It was decided to wage open war against the Head Master. It was next settled that my mother should call on the Rector early next morning, before he received Kamashev's report. She was to ask permission to visit me twice a day in the hospital and then ask him to promise that, if the doctor thought it necessary, I should have leave to go home and stay there, with my parents to look after me, till I had quite recovered. Benis only asked of her not to complain of Kamashev, not to abuse him, and not to allude to his personal dislike and persecution of me. My mother called down Heaven's blessing on the doctor and his wife, and expressed all the gratitude that a mother's heart can feel; and then she went back to her lodgings to rest. Rest was a positive necessity for her: a day filled with such painful anxiety, after traveling twelve days under such conditions with little sleep or food, would have been enough to prostrate even a strong man, and she was a woman, and not in robust health.

But God reveals His power and might in the feeble, and after some hours of sleep, she awoke full of courage and determination. At nine in the morning she was already seated in the Rector's drawing room. He came at once, and his manner clearly showed that he was prejudiced against her. But his mood soon changed, when the sincerity of grief and the eloquence of tears found the way to his heart. Without raising much difficulty, he gave her leave to visit her son in the hospital twice a day and stay there till eight in the evening, but her request that I might leave the school met with more opposition. Tears and entreaties would perhaps have won a second victory, but suddenly the Head Master came in, and the scene changed. The Rector now raised his voice and said that it was an unheard-of proceeding to let Government scholars go home, either on the ground of ill-health, or because they suffered from homesickness. In the former case, it would be an admission that there was insufficient medical attendance and care for the boys when ill, and in the latter, it would be simply absurd: what boy, especially a spoiled boy accustomed to seek only his own amusement, would *not* feel homesick when sent to school? Kamashev at once chimed in and supported the Rector: he said a great deal, and there was much good sense in what he said, and as much ill-nature. He referred to the harm done by women as educators and by mothers who spoiled their children; he spoke of dangerous examples of disrespect, insubordination, presumption, and ingratitude. Finally he said that when the Government spent money on the salaries of the staff and the maintenance of the scholars, it did not intend that the boys should leave the school before passing through the whole curriculum and making themselves competent to serve the State in the teaching profession. He added that the authorities of the school must attach special importance to a boy whose excellent ability and conduct made it likely that he would turn out to be a successful teacher.

This Jesuitical duplicity was too much for my mother: forgetting Benis's warning, she burst out with great warmth and little prudence: "It surprises me that M. Kamashev should praise my son, because he has never ceased, since the poor boy entered the school, to vex and torment him for trifles, to rebuke him when he did not deserve it, and to make fun of him. He has applied to him many insulting nicknames, such as 'crybaby' and 'mama's darling,' which of course have been taken up by all the boys; and this unjust persecution on the part of the Head Master is the only reason why ordinary homesickness has developed into a dangerous illness. I recognize the Head Master as my personal enemy. He usurps power that does not belong to him; he tried to turn me out of the hospital, although I had the Rector's permission. He is a partial judge, and has no right to decide this question!"

The Rector was a good deal disconcerted, but Kamashev retorted angrily that she herself and her unreasonable impetuosity were entirely to blame. "In my absence," he said, "she took advantage of the weakness of my substitute, and constantly took her son home or visited him here. Then she broke off her journey and came back to Kazan, and after two months has come back again. In this way she never gives the boy time to get accustomed to his new position. She herself, and not the severity of his masters, is the cause of his illness; and her present visit will do a great deal of harm, for her son, who was recovering, had a serious relapse early this morning." At these words, my mother cried out and fainted away. The good-natured Rector was horribly frightened and perplexed. The swoon lasted long; it was nearly an hour before she became conscious, and her first words were, "Let me go to my son!" The Rector, very sorry for her and frightened about her, was glad that at least she was not dead—he much feared that she was, as he used to tell afterwards—and he gave a positive order to Kamashev that she was to be admitted at all times to the hospital; and there she accordingly went at once.

The doctor met her there and did his best to calm her fears. He gave her a solemn assurance that my new symptom, fever, was of no importance, being due merely to nervous excitement; it might even have a good influence on my regular attacks. In fact, the first fever-fit was very mild, and though the second was more severe and was followed by others during the next fortnight, yet the hysterical seizures never returned. Nearly the whole of every day my mother spent with me. The Rector visited the hospital several times, and each time that he found her there, showed much kindness to both of us: he could not look without pity at my thin pale face; and the expressive features of my mother, which clearly revealed her thoughts and feelings, also awakened his sympathy. But when Kamashev tried to enter my room next day, she locked the door and would not let him in; and afterwards she asked the Rector to prevent the Head Master from visiting me in her presence. "I cannot control myself," she said, "at the sight of that man, and I am afraid of frightening the patient by an attack such as I had in your house." The Rector, who had a lively recollection of that event, expressed his willingness; and Kamashev, much insulted, ceased coming to see me at all.

Meanwhile the plan of removing me from the school, which had gained strength from the doctor's consent and then been postponed by my fresh illness, was proceeding in due form. My mother wished to begin by discussing the plan with her friends, and went to see M. Knyazhevich. That kind-hearted but rather gruff and positive Serbian disapproved of her purpose. "No, no! my dear lady," he said; "I cannot advise you to take your son and wrap him up in cotton wool, to coddle him and feed him on sugar and carry him off to the country, that he may run about there with the village boys and grow up ignorant and good-for-nothing. You will make nothing of him that way. I tell you frankly that, if I were in your husband's place, I should not allow you to do it." My mother was displeased; she said that she did not intend her son to grow up a dunce and a bumpkin, but she did certainly wish to save his life and restore him to health. She had no further interviews with M. Knyazhevich. Next she turned to a distant relation of my father's who lived at Kazan: his name was Mikheyev, and he was a lawyer. Though he also disapproved of her plan and declined to take any active steps in support of it, he was willing to do one thing she asked—to write a petition for my release, to be submitted to the Governors. In the petition, my mother asked that her son might be restored to her for a time, with a view to the recovery of his health; and she pledged herself to place me again in the school as a Government scholar as soon as I was well. This petition was accompanied by a report from Dr. Benis, in which he said that, in his opinion, it was absolutely necessary to send young Aksakov home to his parents; the country was specially indicated, because my illness was of a kind which nothing but country air and home life could overcome; treatment in the hospital would be quite useless; my attacks threatened to develop into epilepsy, and epilepsy might end in apoplexy or injury to the brain. How far all this was true, I cannot tell, but the doctor was not content to stop there. He asserted that I had some swelling of the knees and a tendency to crookedness in the bones of the leg, and these symptoms called for exercise in the open air and a prolonged course of some syrup—I don't remember its name—which he offered to supply out of the stock of medicines provided by the Government for the school. I believe that all this last part of the report was fictitious: I really had very thick knees, but many children have, and it passes off without treatment. Nevertheless, these trifling external symptoms were treated with great respect in the later stages of this affair.

The business began at a meeting of the Governors. The Rector was in the chair, and the others present were Kamashev and the three senior teachers. Kamashev, who generally settled everything, asserted his influence, and the three teachers sided with him. The Rector could not make up his mind. The majority were for instructing Benis to invite the senior medical officer in the town to a consultation and then to continue his treatment of me; but Benis explained beforehand that he would not carry out such an instruction, and would report to the Governors in favor of letting me go at once, for as soon as the fever had passed off, symptoms had appeared, portending a renewal of the previous attacks. This, indeed, was perfectly true. My poor mother, seeing that things were not going well, became quite desperate. Finally Benis advised my mother to put this request before the Rector—that he should order me to be examined in his presence by the school doctor and other doctors from outside, and that he should be guided by their opinion; and she drove off at once to the Rector's house. Wishing to protect himself from tears and petitions, of which he was heartily weary, the Rector sent a message that he could not possibly receive her that day and hoped she would come back another time. But this rebuff was not the first, and my mother was prepared; she had brought with her a letter, in which she said, "This is my last visit. If you refuse to see me, I will not leave your drawing room till I am turned out. But I do not believe you will behave so harshly to an unhappy mother." The Rector could not help himself. He emerged into the drawing room, and again he was not proof against the expression of genuine grief and even despair. He pledged his word to carry out all my mother's wishes, and he kept his word. The very next day the Governors of the school passed a motion in perfect agreement with Benis's suggestion and my mother's request. But the Rector himself was the only person who was aware of this: everyone else thought that Benis would resent an examination by outside doctors, and they were convinced that these doctors would disagree with Benis.

Two of the leading physicians in the town were called in. Benis, confident that they would concur in his opinion, waited calmly for the issue of events, and his confidence did something to calm my mother, who tried in her turn to soothe me. She repeated to me in minute detail all she had done and all she had said, and tried to convince me that, in spite of obstacles, she had not given up hope of success. I could share this hope only at times and not for long: deliverance from my stone prison, as I called the school, and restoration to my home in the country seemed to me bliss beyond attainment and beyond possibility. The choice of doctors involved much correspondence with the authorities; and the Rector, urged by Kamashev, ordered that I should be discharged from hospital, the fever having entirely left me. Benis was forced to give his consent. So I went back to Upadishevsky's dormitory, where I found my bed empty. After a considerable spell of freedom in the peace and quiet of the sick room, I disliked more than ever the regular rules and constant noise of school life; and also the move struck me as a bad sign, unfavorable to my hopes of release. I saw my mother daily, but only in the general reception room and not for long. All this brought depression back upon me, and my attacks began again, as violent as before, as if there had been no cessation of them. But this painful situation did not last long, thank God!

Just a week after my return, when supper was over and the boys came down to the dormitories and began to undress, Yevseich pushed into my hand a note from my mother and said, "Don't let anyone see you reading this!" My mother told me not to get up next morning; I was to tell Upadishevsky that my legs, and especially my knees, were aching, and to ask sick-leave to the hospital. I was told to burn the note, and I did so at once. I was very much surprised by these instructions, for I was quite unaccustomed to tell lies, and my mother never passed over untruths without punishment. Though I had a dim suspicion in the back of my head that this lie would help to set me free from school, yet I lay awake a long time; I was unhappy at the thought that tomorrow I must tell an untruth and that Upadishevsky and the doctor would at once see through it and detect me. But when Yevseich woke me next morning, I told him that my legs were aching and that I wished to return to the hospital. A suppressed smile curled the lips of my good Yevseich as he went off to inform Upadishevsky. To my surprise Upadishevsky took it very coolly. "Very well," he said, "let him stay in bed. I shall just take the boys upstairs and then come back for him and take him off to the hospital." But the boys would not leave me in peace, and a number of them, pulling off the coverlet which I had purposely drawn over my head, asked me why I did not get up. Blushing and confused, I was forced to repeat my lie several times. They laughed and said, "You're shamming, you're too lazy to work, you like hospital better." Then the crowd of noisy boys fell in and marched upstairs in order. Upadishevsky soon came back and, without asking any questions about my ailment, took me to the hospital and handed me over to the charge of Ritter, the assistant-surgeon, and the superintendent. My old room was assigned to me, and at nine o'clock Benis came. On beginning his examination, he put this leading question, "I suppose you feel pain in the legs? I quite expected it." Then he made the superintendent and the assistant-surgeon look at my knees and added, "See how swollen they are in one week, and the inflammation is worse." There was not the least change in the state of my knees, and I felt no inflammation, but I noticed with surprise that there seemed to be a general conspiracy to keep up the pretence. I was even more surprised when my mother arrived soon after Benis and discussed quite calmly with him and the others my new and fictitious symptoms. When we were alone, I looked at her with wonder and asked what it all meant. She took me in her arms and said, "My dear, we cannot help it. It is the only way; it is what Benis told us to do. You will soon be examined by the other doctors, and you must tell them that you have pains in your legs. Dr. Benis is positive that this will secure your discharge." A ray of hope flashed before my mind, though I saw no special reason to rely upon it. Two days later, my mother told me at night that the examination would take place the next day; she repeated all that I was to say about my afflicted legs and urged me to answer boldly and without hesitation.

At eleven the next day a whole party entered my room— the Rector, the Head Master, Benis and two strange doctors, the three teachers who were members of the governing body, and Upadishevsky. They filled my room, which was not large; chairs were placed for them all, and they all sat solemnly down beside my bed. I was so confused that I began at once to feel faint, but I soon recovered without any medicine and listened, while Benis told his colleagues the history of my illness, sometimes speaking in Latin but chiefly in Russian. He referred again and again to Upadishevsky, and the others cross-examined the dormitory master on the spot. Yevseich also was summoned, and several questions were put to him about my state of health before I entered the school. I too had to answer a great many inquiries; the doctors came up to my bed again and again, sounded my chest and stomach, felt my pulse, and looked at my tongue. When my knees and leg bones came under consideration, all three of them came round me, and all three suddenly began to prod me in the part supposed to be affected; they talked very earnestly and got very excited. I remember that they often repeated the terms "serum," "lymphs," "scorbutic habit." The examination lasted for an hour at least, and I was quite worn out by it, but it ended at last, and I fell asleep as soon as they had all gone.

When I woke, my mother was sitting by me, and my dinner was standing cold on the table. My mother was hopeful, but knew nothing yet for certain. She went off immediately to call on Benis, and when she returned in two hours her face was radiant with happiness. The doctors had gone straight from my room to a meeting of the Governors, where they all signed a certificate, to this effect: "In complete agreement with the opinion of Dr. Benis, we consider it absolutely necessary that the Government scholar, Aksakov, should be sent home to the country, to be cared for by his parents. A syrup has already been prescribed for the patient, but we think it as well to add certain other medicines, to be followed by a course of cold baths to recuperate his strength." The Rector gave his consent in plain terms, and the three teachers followed his example; only Kamashev would not budge, and refused to sign the minutes,* but that did no harm.

And so the desired event, which for so long had seemed a mere castle in the air, really came to pass. My mother was radiant with bliss; she laughed and cried and embraced everybody, especially Upadishevsky and Yevseich, and she thanked God. I was so happy at times I could not believe in my happiness: I thought it all a beautiful dream and feared to wake up. I clasped my mother close and asked if it was really true. She sat with me longer than usual that evening, till Upadishevsky came in more than once, to ask her to go. Kamashev behaved like himself to the last: he proposed to the Governors to require my mother, in view of the five months I had spent at the school, to refund the whole cost of my maintenance and education. But the Rector did not agree. He said that I was not being expelled but only sent home for convalescence. Three days after the consultation

---

* Copies of all the papers were long preserved in our house. (Author's note)

the Governors summoned my mother to appear before them and made her sign a promise to send me back when I was well; then they gave her leave to take me. She came straight from the meeting to visit the hospital for the last time; Yevseich had dressed me in my own clothes, returning my uniform and books and all other Government property. We said good-bye to Upadishevsky and to the hospital superintendent with tears of ardent gratitude. Then my mother took my hand, and she and Yevseich brought me out upon the steps.

I gave a cry of joyful surprise. The carriage from home was standing in front of the steps, drawn by four of our own horses bred at Aksakovo; I knew the coachman on the box, and I knew the postilion still better, for he used always to supply me with worms for bait. Theodore and Yevseich placed me at my mother's side in the old carriage, and we drove off to our lodgings. In spite of the joy which filled or, I might say, intoxicated my heart, I cried so when taking leave of Upadishevsky that I went on crying even in the carriage. And surely this good man's unselfish kindness to us who had been mere strangers, and his tender sympathy which did not shrink from self-sacrifice, deserved the truest gratitude; and it should be added that his many years of service at the school could not fail to accustom him to cases of the kind, and there are few hearts that are not hardened by custom. At our lodgings, Parasha was awaiting me with tears of joy, and the lady of the house, our old acquaintance Mme. Aristov, showed in the same way the interest she took in our situation.

That same evening my mother and I called on Dr. Benis, to thank him and say good-bye. I must do full justice to him too: for some reason he passed in the town for a cold, selfish man, but his conduct to us was obliging and disinterested.

He would not take one penny from us and even refused the present which my mother offered him as a token of our obligations; of course she repaid the twenty-five rubles that he had paid as consultation fee to each of the doctors who had examined me. All she could do was to thank Benis with words and tears and prayers for his welfare; and she did this with such warmth and sincerity that he and his wife were deeply touched. So far as I was concerned, I was somehow not touched; and though I knew very well that I owed my deliverance from school to Benis alone, I shed no tears, and my expression of thanks was so languid and trivial that my mother scolded me afterwards. Early the next day we went to the Cathedral and then to the church of Our Lady of Kazan and offered thankful prayers. We called on the Rector, but he was either away from home or unwilling to receive us. On returning home, we found Upadishevsky, who had come for one more parting interview. He also refused to accept any token of thanks. His answer to my mother was short and clear: "Please don't insult me, Sofya Nikolaevna." I did not part with him as I had parted with the doctor. I cried so terribly that for a long time I could not be stopped; and one of the old attacks seemed to be coming on, when my excitement was soothed by some new drops. I ought say of this medicine that three times during these days it was successful in arresting a fainting-fit. When Upadishevsky left, we had a hasty dinner and then set to work at once on our packing. We were afraid to stay in Kazan, and each hour before our departure seemed like a long day. By evening all was ready. The evening set in warm, a real summer evening, and my mother and I went to bed in the carriage. At dawn the horses were put in very quietly, and I was still asleep, when we drove slowly out of Kazan.

When I awoke, bright sunlight was pouring into the carriage. Parasha was asleep; my mother was sitting beside me, weeping tears of joy and gratitude to God; and her eyes showed her feeling so clearly that any spectator of her tears would have rejoiced and not grieved. She embraced her darling child, and a torrent of tender words and caresses showed what she was feeling. It was the 19th of May, my sister's birthday. It was a real May day; the spring morning was warm, even hot, and flooded all the landscape with burning light. The green fields of young corn, the meadows and woods, peeped in at the carriage windows; I felt such a desire to survey the whole wide prospect that I asked to have the carriage stopped. Then I sprang out, and began to run and jump like a playful child of five, while my mother watched me with delight from the carriage. For the first time, I felt that I was really free. I embraced Yevseich and Theodore; I exchanged greetings with the coachman and postilion, and the latter found time to tell me that when he left Aksakovo the fish were beginning "to bite fine." Next I greeted all the horses: Yevseich held me up in his arms while I patted each of them. There were six of them, a splendid team of bays and dark-browns, of a breed which has long been quite extinct; but twenty years ago, it was still remembered and often spoken of in the Province of Orenburg. They were big horses, standing over sixteen hands high, and strong beyond belief. They generally trotted but could gallop without distress, and they never tired; they used often to draw a heavy carriage eighty or ninety versts in a day.

Ah, how delighted I was! When I was obliged to get back into the carriage, I stuck my head out of the window and kept it there till we reached our halting-place, greeting everything we passed with cries of joy. At last a streak of water sparkled before us: this was the Myosha, not a very large river, but deep and abounding with fish. A rather crazy raft worked by a rope crossed it; and we took a long time to get over. Only one pair of horses could cross at a time, and the carriage could hardly be managed at all: even when all the heavy trunks were taken off it, it made the raft sink low in the water. My mother and I crossed first. The far side was covered with trees and bushes, whose fragrant blossoms drove me nearly mad with delight. Our postilion was very fond of fishing and had brought with him from home a rod and line ready for all emergencies. This was quickly unfastened from its place under the carriage, and while the horses were crossing, I was fishing, with bread for bait, and pulling out roach. Except the Dyoma, I never saw a river better stocked than the Myosha; the fish swarmed in it and took as fast as you could bait your line and throw it back. Is it any wonder that to me, delivered from the prison of school, this halt seemed like heaven?

On the riverbank behind us there was a gentleman's estate, where we got hay and oats, a chicken and eggs, and other necessary provisions. Yevseich was a bit of a cook, and he cooked us a splendid dinner on a gridiron. The fish, fried in a pan, tasted excellent. We had driven thirty versts from Kazan, and we stopped four hours before starting again. Clouds came up, thunder began to roll, the ground was sprinkled with rain, the heat and dust disappeared. We started at a slow pace, but afterwards trotted so fast that we covered ten versts in an hour. The sky soon cleared, and a splendid sun dried up the traces of rain. We drove on forty versts farther and camped out for the night, having procured all we needed at our last stop. A fresh supply of pleasures and enjoyments for me! The horses were taken out and hobbled and allowed to crop the juicy young grass; a bright fire was lit, and the traveling samovar—really a large teapot with a funnel—was placed on it. A leather rug was spread out beside the carriage, the canteen was brought out, and tea served. How good it was in the fresh evening air! In two hours the horses had cooled down and were watered; their nosebags were opened and fastened either to the carriage pole or to posts driven into the ground; and then the horses were let loose upon the oats. My mother and I and Parasha lay down in the carriage, and as I sank into a delicious sleep, I listened to the horses munching their oats and snorting when the dusty particles got into their nostrils.

Early next day we crossed the Kama, which was still in flood, a little above Shuran. I was afraid, as I am still, to cross a great river; and a tolerable breeze was blowing that day. There was a large new ferryboat, on which room was found for all our horses and the carriage. Parasha and I were shut up inside the carriage, with the blinds down, to prevent my seeing the rushing water; I tied a handkerchief round my head as well; yet even then I shook with fear till we had got across. But there were no unpleasant consequences. We landed at Murzikha, and my mother hunted up the fishermen who had guided her over the ice; she had brought handsome presents for them all, and the presents were received with no surprise but with pleasure and gratitude. Fifteen versts brought us to our next halt. And so our journey went on, till on the fifth day we arrived at Baitugan, a village on the river Sok (where we spent a night) and not more than twenty versts from Aksakovo. Though this is a good river for fishing, my mother feared the evening damp and would not allow me to go, but our postilion took a run to the riverside and came back with some perch and roach. By rising at dawn as usual, we avoided stopping at Neklyudovo where relations of my grandmother lived; they were asleep when we passed, and so were we. Four versts from Aksakovo, just where our estate begins, I woke up suddenly, as if I had been roused on purpose; we drove on between the two woods and came out on the slope of the hill. From there we were bound soon to see Aksakovo— the large pond and the mill, the long line of peasants' huts, our house and the birch woods beside it. I kept asking the coachman whether he could see it, and at last he bent down to the front window and said, "There is our Aksakovo, as clear as if it lay in the palm of one's hand!" Then I begged so eagerly to sit on the box beside the coachman that my mother could not refuse me. I shall not try to describe what I felt when I saw my dear Aksakovo. Human language has no words adequate to express such feelings!

I continued throughout my life to feel, when approaching Aksakovo, the same emotion as I did then. But some years ago I was getting near the place after an absence of twelve years. Again it was early morning; my heart beat fast with expectation, and I hoped to feel the happy excitement of former days. I called up the dear old times, and a swarm of memories came round me. Alas! they brought no happiness to my heart but only pain and suffering, and I felt heavy and sad beyond expression. Like the magician, who sought in vain to hide from the spirits he had called up but could not control, so I did not know how to banish my recollections and lay the storm of my troubled heart. Old bottles will not hold new wine, and old hearts are unfit to bear the feelings of youth. But *then*—ah, what were my feelings *then*!

Several times I felt the oppression on my chest and was pretty near falling, but I said nothing and held tight to the rail of the box and pressed against the coachman, and the trouble passed off naturally. The carriage rolled quickly down the hill and crossed the rickety bridge over the river.

We nearly stuck in a swampy place, but our strong horses pulled the carriage through it, and we passed the reed beds, the pond, and the village. And there was our house at last, and standing on the steps were my father and my dear little sister. When we drove up, she clapped her little hands and screamed out, "Brother Seryozha is on the box!" My aunt hurried out, bringing my brother; and my baby sister was carried out by her nurse. How many embraces and kisses! How many questions and answers! How much happiness! All the outdoor servants collected, and even the laborers who happened to be at home, and a crowd of boys and girls from the village. My father was delighted. He was doubtful whether it would be possible to get me away from school; and we were too busy during our last week in Kazan to let him know what was happening.

2

✧

A Year in the Country

The first days were days of unthinking and unresting activity. My earliest visit was paid to my pigeons and the two hawks that had lived through the winter. Then I ran round to every dear and familiar spot, and there were plenty of them. Round the house, in the garden and kitchen-garden, and in the wood with the jackdaws' nests near the house, my sister kept constantly at my side and held my hand; sometimes she even pointed out to me, as if I were a stranger, some alteration which I had missed by my absence—for instance, a steaming hotbed, very large and high, planted with melons and gourds. We went together to the storeroom, where some pretty boxes were kept; they were made of copper or iron and adorned with carved ivory, and contained a number of specimens and fossils presented to my mother long ago by some friend who held an important position in the mines. We paid a visit also to the cellar, where Pelageya, the housekeeper, feasted us on cool thick cream and brown bread.

To the river and across the river my sister might not go with me, and Yevseich took her place for the time. He and

I went over the gangway to the first island, where our sum-
mer-kitchen was, and a wide bark floor where the wheat
was dried after it was washed clean. This little island was
surrounded on two sides by the old channel of the river,
which was now overgrown with osiers and beginning to dry
up. We crossed this channel on planks and came at once to
the other island. It was larger, and the old channel which
surrounded it on one side was still deep and clear. This
was a favorite spot with my aunt Tatyana; it was divided
in the middle by a lime avenue, and birches grew all along
the river bank. My grandfather must have had a fancy for
the place in old days, for he planted the trees there long
before the birth of his youngest daughter, Tanyusha* as he
used to call her; the trees were now fifty years old, and she
was thirty-five. Like all her sisters, my aunt had received
no education, but she loved nature and kept in her heart a
kind of leaning towards culture. She possessed a few stray
books, chiefly old novels, probably procured for her by her
brother, and some plays. Of course, I read them all through,
with permission or without permission; I remember in par-
ticular a kind of vaudeville called *A Trifle for the Stage*. My
aunt was fond of sitting on the island, where she read a book
and fished in the deep water of the old channel. On many
of the birch trees she had carved her own name and various dates, and even verses from her songbook. How I loved
this island! How pleasant it was in summer heat to sit there
in the cool shade with the water all round! On one side
the new cutting from the milldam joined the stream that
raced from under the mill wheel; and on the other side the
old channel of the Buguruslan, then deep and clear, made
a bend round the island. To this day my heart is strongly

* A pet-name for Tatyana.

stirred when I recall the summer afternoons I spent there. Now, all is changed. The old channel is almost dry; a fresh cutting carries away the water from the pond in another direction; the osiers and alders have spread everywhere; and the island, though it keeps the name, no longer deserves it. In a loose sense, indeed, the name may be applied to the whole plot of land extending to the milldam.

When I had admired the island sufficiently, had examined each tree and read all my aunt's inscriptions, and had looked long enough at the chub and carp darting below me or hanging motionless in the water—then I started off with Yevseich for the mill; but first I paid hasty visits to two other spots, "Antony's gangway" where I used to catch gudgeon, and the forge where I liked to watch the red-hot iron and the sparks leaping from under the hammer. When at last the expanse of the pond opened out before me with its green reeds and burdock leaves, and the long milldam overgrown with young alder and teeming with a bird and fish population of its own, I was mute with wonder and delight and stood there some minutes, as if rooted to the ground. I was a favorite with the miller, who was nicknamed Boltunyonok,* and he had prepared a surprise for me. Knowing that I was sure to come, he had set some wire lines among the weed for pike and left them unvisited till I came. Now he made Yevseich and me get into a boat and rowed us to the place; the water was very shallow, and I was not frightened this time. I drew up each line myself, and on one of them was a large pike, which I pulled out with Yevseich to help me, and carried in triumph all the way home in my hands.

Two days later my father took me further afield to fish; he also drove with me to "Antony's dyke," where an active

* "Little chatterbox"; *boltun* = chatterbox.

spring spouted from the top of a hill, making a foaming waterfall; to Koloda, where the water ran from a spring into wooden troughs ready to receive it; to the Mordov dyke, where a spring burst out of a rocky fissure at the foot of the hill; to the lime-tree wood, and the "Sacred Wood,"* and the place between them where the beehives were kept. The old bee-man, another great friend of mine, lived there summer and winter in a low turf hut; he had a tomcat called Alka and a tabby called Sonya, which he had named, as a compliment, after my father and mother.

Such were the pleasant occupations that took up my time during the first fortnight after our arrival at Aksakovo. I need not say how happy my mother was when she saw me cheerful and enterprising and, to all appearance, well. Before leaving Kazan, in order to prevent my life in the country being spent in complete idleness, she had procured copies of the textbooks used in the school. She never forgot that, if by God's mercy I recovered my health, I must be sent back to school at the end of a year; and she set apart two or three hours a day in which I was to review what I had learned and practice writing and read aloud to her various books suitable to my age. I carried out this plan very willingly, and my outdoor amusements pleased me all the better after my tasks. I also began again to teach my dear little sister and pupil to read; and this time my efforts were crowned with complete success.

I said above that I was apparently quite well, but it did not in fact turn out quite so. It is true that I had not a single seizure after leaving school, and the feeling of oppression and palpitation passed away on our journey, and there was

* A wood preserved from the ravages of thieves by a religious service celebrated by the priest on the spot.

no return of these symptoms at home. But I now became excessively restless and began to talk in my sleep every night. At first my mother attached no importance at all to this, attributing it to over-exercise and the liveliness of a child's impressions; this was all the more natural, because I had often talked in my sleep before I went to school, and many children are apt to do so. But now the thing began by degrees to assume a different character.

In the first place, I began to talk every night, and several times on some nights, and to talk very excitedly. In the second place, I began also to cry and sob in my sleep, to jump out of bed and try to walk out of the room. I slept with my parents in their bedroom, and my bed was close to theirs. The door was now locked on the inside, and Pelageya the housekeeper slept in the passage outside the door, to make it impossible for me to leave the room. My nocturnal distress grew worse every day, or rather every night, till at last it bore an evident resemblance to the fits from which I used to suffer, during the day only, at school: once again I cried and sobbed till I became unconscious, and this was followed by ordinary sound sleep. But these fresh attacks by night were much more violent and alarming than what I had experienced before, and there was more variety in the symptoms. Sometimes I cried quietly and moaned, with hands always clenched against my chest and inarticulate muttering; this went on for whole hours and passed into spasmodic and furious movements in case an attempt was made to wake me. As time went on, these attempts were given up. When I was tired out by tears and sobbing, I went quietly to sleep. But it was very difficult, especially at first, for the bystanders to look on at such suffering without trying to wake me and afford me some relief. I was told afterwards that not only my mother, who suffered terribly at the sight, but my father and my aunt and all my attendants broke down and could not witness my distressing symptoms without tears. At other times I sprang to my feet with a piercing cry and stared wildly round, repeating again and again disjointed and meaningless phrases, such as, "Let me go!"—"Go away!"—"I can't!"—"Where is he?"—"Where shall I go?" Then I dashed to the door or window or corners of the room, trying to get past, and battering the wall with hands and feet. At such times I was so strong that two or three people could not hold me, and I dragged them about the room, with the sweat pouring from me. This kind of attack always ended with a severe fainting fit, in the course of which it was hard to determine whether I was still breathing; the swoon by degrees passed off into sleep, rather disturbed at first, but then sound and quiet, and sometimes lasting till nine in the morning. After such a night I woke up as fresh and lively as if I had been peacefully asleep all the time; and though the furious excitement and exertion left me rather weak and pale, these symptoms soon passed off, and I was quite cheerful all day, learning my lessons, running about, and giving myself up to my amusements. On waking, I had no clear recollection that anything had happened; sometimes I fancied vaguely that I had dreamed of something falling upon me and smothering me, or of monsters pursuing me; sometimes, when the people holding me could not help coaxing me with kind words to lie down and be quiet, their efforts roused me for an instant to a sense of reality. Then, when I was wide awake next morning, I remembered waking for some reason in the night, to find my parents and others standing by my bed, while the nightingales sang in the bushes under the windows and the corncrakes cried across the river.

My mother was at her wits' end; she was specially alarmed by the way in which my face was convulsed and I foamed at the mouth, while unconscious. These were ominous signs; and the idea that my trouble might really be that epilepsy, which Yevseich had foretold in his letter long before, filled her with horror. She ceased to give me the drops prescribed by Dr. Benis; the medicine for purifying the blood, which had been supplied from the Government stock of drugs, she never used at all, though Benis advised that it should be tried; he suspected scrofula, which I never had. She allowed me to bathe in the river, thinking that bathing might make me stronger; but, though I enjoyed it exceedingly, it did me no good. Next my mother had recourse to Benis: she sent him a description of the course of my illness, a description so admirable that the doctor was charmed by it; he thanked her for it and sent me some pills and a kind of tea, and prescribed a diet. All his directions were precisely carried out, but the illness was not relieved. On the contrary, the attacks became more obstinate, and I grew weaker. The medicines were now given up, and the "wise women" and "wise men" of the countryside were tried. They all agreed that I was bewitched and had been "overlooked" by someone; they tried baths and ointments and fumigations, but all to no purpose.

I am not in the least opposed to popular medicine. I believe in it, especially in connection with mesmerism; and I have long ago renounced the contemptuous view which many take of it, from their superior position of enlightenment and science. I have seen so many remarkable and convincing cases that I cannot question the efficacy of many of the remedies used by the people. But they did me no good then, perhaps because they did not suit my ailment or perhaps because my mother would not allow any but external applications to be tried. I remember, however, that on the advice of a lady who lived near us I took powdered fern for a long time; only the youngest sprouts were used, those which look like a comb and spring immediately from the root, between the large indented leaves of the plant. But the fern also did no good. In the end, the commonest of all medicines was tried; it had been constantly used in our house in my grandparents' time, and my aunt had often suggested it; but my mother had a prejudice against it, and for long would not hear of its being tried. It was called "fit-drops" or "storax-drops," because the resin of storax was the chief ingredient; ten drops were poured into half a glass of water, and the water turned as white as milk. The number of drops was increased by two each day, till twenty-five were taken at one dose; it was always given at night. After twenty-five drops had been reached, the dose was lessened by two drops each day till it finally came down to ten. The very first dose did me good, and in a month the illness had completely disappeared and never returned. I went on bathing all the time and ate just what I pleased. What a noise it would have made, if some famous doctor had cured me with such marvelous success! What a relief it was to my poor mother and father and all the household, especially to Pelageya the housekeeper, who was constantly occupied with me during the attacks, beginning to tell me fairy stories as soon as I went to bed, and going on with them even after I fell asleep. My mother was as happy as if she had rescued me from school a second time. My case shows how often we go far afield in search of healing, when it is close beside us all the time. I shall now go back a little in the course of my narrative.

In spite of the alarming nature of my illness, I went on all the time with my lessons and outdoor amusements also;

only, when the attacks became more severe, I was more moderate in the amount of exercise I took, and my mother kept a careful eye on me and would not let me go far away or for long. Every morning before the great heat came on, I went out with Yevseich to fish. Our very best fishing was in the garden, and almost under our windows, because there was a mill and a very large pond below Aksakovo in the village of Kivatsky, and the overflow caused by the dam extended nearly as far up as our garden. Every sportsman knows how good the fishing is under such conditions. Now for the first time I became acquainted with the fisherman's chief delight—the catching of large fish. Up till then I had caught only roach, perch, and gudgeon; it is true that the two former fish often attain considerable size, but for some reason, I never happened to hook a very large one; and if I had, I could not have landed it, as I used thin lines and small hooks. But now Yevseich plaited two lines for me, each of twenty horsehairs, attached stout hooks to them, and tied the lines to strong rods; then he took his own line as well, and guided me through the garden to a pool which he kept a secret from others and which he called "The Golden Pool." He baited my hook with a piece of brown breadcrumb about the size of a large hazelnut and cast my line right under a bush in the deep water, while he dropped his own by the bank near the weed and rushes. I sat quietly, never daring to take my eyes off my float as it swayed gently up and down in the eddy that formed under the bank. Before long, Yevseich suddenly sprang up and cried out, "I've got him, *batyushka*";* then he began to struggle with a big fish, holding the rod in both hands. Yevseich had no idea of sci-

---

* The word means "father," but is used as a general title of respect or affection.

entific fishing—he merely pulled with all his might, trying to jerk the fish out over his shoulder. But the fish had probably got fixed behind some weed or rushes; the rod was no more than a stick, and the line broke, so that we did not even see what sort of a fish it was. Yevseich was much excited; I too, as I watched him, was almost shaking. He vowed that it was the largest fish he had ever hooked in his life, but it was probably a carp or chub of ordinary size, which seemed so heavy to him because it had got entangled in the weed. Then he shook free my other line and cast it as quickly as he could into the same spot. "I believe I was a little too hasty," he said. "Next time I won't pull so hard," and down he sat on the grass, to wait for a second bite; but none came.

My chance came next, and fortune resolved to do me a good turn. My float began gradually to rise on end and fall again; then it remained on end and finally disappeared under water. I struck, and a very large fish began to move heavily, as if reluctantly, through the water. When Yevseich ran to my aid and caught hold of my rod, I remembered what he had just said, and I told him again and again not to pull so hard. At last, as the rod, which I never let go, was not very supple,* and the line was new and strong, we landed somehow by our united efforts a very large carp. Yevseich fell on it at full length, crying out, "Now we've got him, my little falcon. He won't escape now!" In my joy I shook like a man in a fever—indeed this often happened afterwards when I caught a large fish; for long I could not calm down, but kept constantly running to look at my prize, as it lay on the grassy bank at a safe distance from the water. We threw

---

* In order to land big fish, a supple rod is generally much better than a stiff one. But in this case, contrary to all the rules of art, the fish was jerked out over the shoulder, and therefore the stiff rod did good service, as the line was tough enough to support the fish. (Author's note)

in the line again, but the fish had ceased to take, and half an hour later we went home, as I had only leave to be out a short time. This early success confirmed once for all my passion for fishing. We tied the carp to a branch, and I carried it home to show my father, who liked to fish at times himself. In those days it was not our custom at Aksakovo to weigh big fish, but I believe that I never afterwards caught so large a carp, and that it weighed at least seven pounds.

My father sometimes took me with him when he went out shooting, but he went very seldom. I took a strong interest in the proceedings, and these expeditions were red-letter days for me, although my share was confined to performing the duties of a retriever: I mean that I ran to pick up the dead birds and handed them to my father. I might not even hold the gun. But in the summer holidays three years later— I shall describe this period when I come to it—I fired a gun for the first time, and my fate was fixed; all other sports, even fishing, lost their charm in my eyes, and I became and remained throughout life a passionate lover of the gun.

August was ending before I was quite well again, and the large fish had long ceased to take, but I managed to pull out some of considerable size and, as a matter of course, lost twice as many; the perch-fishing, on the other hand, was still at its best. Besides, I was much interested at that time in hawking. As early as July, the old hawks were taken out in pursuit of quails, and the young birds taken from the nest had long been in training. The sport was carried on with great success. The old hawks were managed by Mazan and Tanaichonok, the young ones by Theodore and Yevseich. I had a little hawk of my own, very well trained, with which I caught sparrows and other small birds. I sometimes drove to the fields on a long car with one of the falconers, most often with Yevseich, and I liked to watch the pursuit of the fat autumn quails and landrails. And so I passed the summer and beginning of autumn, constantly engaged in country occupations and amusements, among which I may reckon expeditions to pick berries and, later in the year, mushrooms.*

My mother had no taste for such expeditions and could seldom be persuaded to drive with my father and me to field or forest. I remember, however, that she was sometimes tempted out to the fallow lands near the house by the wild strawberries which grew there in wonderful profusion in those days; she was very fond of them and thought them good for her health. Occasionally we drove in a family party to the picturesque springs in the hills and drank tea in the shade of the birches; but my mother was bored beyond endurance by picking mushrooms, though my father and aunt were very fond of it, and I shared their taste. But the worst thing of all was that my mother did not love our dear Aksakovo. In her view, its position was low and damp—she was right there to some extent; the smell from the pond and milldam was repulsive; and the water of the springs was chalky and hard. She considered all the conditions positively dangerous to her health, and though there was much truth in her views, there was also much prejudice and exaggeration. It must be remembered that she was born and grew up in a town and would have found the country anywhere lacking in interest. My father and I listened with mortification to the eloquent invectives that she often aimed at Aksakovo, and though we did not venture to defend it,

* I did not then foresee that picking mushrooms would provide one of the standing amusements of my old age. In gratitude for this, I long ago took a fancy—and I do not yet give it up—of writing a little book about mushrooms and the pleasure of picking them. (Author's note)

[Aksakov did write an article on the subject, which is included in his works.]

our hearts were not convinced. Although my mother lived in the country, she did not adopt country ways: she occupied herself with her children, or read, or carried on an active correspondence with former acquaintances, most of them notable people, who, after visiting Ufa or living there for a short time, had kept a lasting feeling of friendship and respect for my mother. She also liked to read medical books, Buchan's *Domestic Medicine* being her chief stand-by; while nursing her sick father for several years, she had become used to reading books of this kind. She kept a medicine chest in the house and treated sick people herself, and not only those on our own estate, so that not a few patients used to be brought from the surrounding villages; in this good work my father gave her his active assistance. To the management of the household she gave hardly any attention.

Autumn now came on, and my outdoor amusements, one after another ceased to be possible. The days grew short and dark; rain and cold soon drove everyone indoors, and I began to spend more time with my mother and to do more lessons in the shape of reading aloud and writing. In the long evenings, my father used to read to us, and occasionally my mother, who was a remarkably good reader. Though my father had not acquired the habit of reading in his early life at home—my grandparents had no books except almanacs and some pamphlets recommending "Haarlem Drops" and "The Elixir of Life"—yet he had a natural taste for literature, as is proved by a very large collection of songs and other verses of that day, copied out by him with his own hand, which is still in my possession. My mother was able to develop this natural taste, and so the readings went on every evening and interested us all. It gives me keen pleasure to recall these evenings, at which my aunt Tatyana was always present. The enjoyment of reading was enhanced by roasted chestnuts, of which my mother was very fond, though they were very bad for her. A copper box containing the chestnuts made its appearance each evening; and nut-crackers and bits of stick were brought in to crack the chest-nuts and open them with.* But as soon as my interest was excited by the reading, I resented the extra entertainment, because it distracted attention and made it difficult to listen. When my mother was in a happy frame of mind and felt bet-ter than usual, her gaiety was infectious; she laughed a great deal and made us laugh too. There were two stories in par-ticular, *Francicico Petroccio* and *The Adventures of Ilya Bendel*, so silly in themselves and so absurdly translated into bad Russian that they excited our hearty laughter; and then my mother's lively and pointed comments worked us up to such a state that we all literally rocked in a paroxysm of merri-ment, which stopped the reading for some time. But there were also books that excited keen interest and sympathy, and even brought tears to the eyes of the listeners.

The approach of winter with its first snow showers and slight frosts made it possible for me to go back for a time to my outdoor amusements. We walked up hares, the large grey kind and the white, over the snow. My father took me with him, and we were accompanied by a miscellaneous crowd of beaters. The method was to place nets almost all round a hare lying in her form; then the beaters with loud shouts moved forward along the open space, till the fright-ened hare sprang up and got entangled in the netting. I ran

---

* The history of this box is worth recording. When my mother was married in 1788, it held her ribbons and laces; in the nineties and as late as 1801, it was our receptacle for roasted chestnuts; in 1807 it con-tained more than 100,000 rubles in notes and bills, and diamonds and pearls worth a great sum; and now it lies under my son's writing-table, crammed with old papers. (Author's note)

too, and, as may be guessed, made more noise and got more excited than anyone. I was very fond of this amusement and liked to talk about it with my father. When my mother was busy over something and found my constant questions troublesome, or when she was not feeling well, she often sent me off to my father with the words, "Go and talk to him about your dear hares!"—and then we two had endless conversations on the subject. Another great occupation of mine was to lay traps for small animals—martens, ermines, and stoats. The soft pretty skins of my victims were hung up as trophies by my bed.

But soon heavy snowstorms began, the ground was covered with deep drifts, and all my outdoor pursuits came to an end for good. A winter snowstorm is a sad and even alarming sight, not only to the wanderer on the steppe, but also to those who sit warm indoors. The snow covers the windows, blows in through the doors, and obliterates all the paths from the house to the servants' cottages, so that they have to be dug out; at forty paces off a man is invisible. At last the snowdrifts become so huge that one cannot believe they will ever disappear, and a feeling of depression is inevitable. Dwellers in the capitals can have no conception of this, but country people will understand and share my feeling. I was confined to the house for good and all; nothing would induce my mother to let me go out with my father on his expeditions to the river. He sometimes went in a sledge to places by a ford, where a barrier or close hedge of stakes, with wicker traps in the middle, had been stuck in where the stream ran deep. Between Christmas and Epiphany, or even earlier, burbot began to get caught in these traps, and some of them were very large. They were brought to the house stiff with the hard frost, and thrown into a large trough full of water; then the fat, mottled, dark-green fish began to thaw by degrees, to splash, and to move their tails covered over with soft down. I stood long beside the trough, admiring their movements, and starting back each time that the drops of water flew from their fins or tails. My father kept a number of these captives in large tanks, and soup made out of them or, still better, pies made out of their livers appeared nearly every day at our table, till we all got heartily tired of them. When they ceased to be popular, they became an occasional dish, and the whole stock was exhausted before the end of Lent.

As I have said already, my mother had formerly lived in a town; she had also suffered much oppression and sadness in her childhood and early youth; and then she had gained what may be called some external contact with culture by the reading of books and by acquaintance with people of intelligence and education, according to the standards of those days—a contact which often arouses a kind of pride and contempt for the simple life of the poor. From all these causes combined, she did not understand and did not like the dances of the people, or their songs at weddings and festivals, or their Christmas revels; she did not even know much about them. She was therefore very unwilling to give her consent when my aunt begged that I might have leave to watch the servants acting. My aunt herself, who had grown up in the country, had a strong taste for everything of the kind: she sometimes got up singing and acting in her own room, and the sweet enchanting sounds of the songs native to the people, as they floated to my ear from two rooms off, filled me with excitement and gave me thoughts which I could not fully understand. I was very much vexed that I was not allowed even to be present at the acting, far less to take part in it, and as a consequence of this strict prohibition, I was tempted at last to deceive my wise mother whom

I loved so well. I began, of course, by begging to go, and besieged my mother with questions, asking why she objected
to my looking on. She answered positively and sternly. "A
great deal that goes on there is silly and repulsive and undesirable, and you have no business to hear or see such things,
because you are still a child, unable to distinguish good
from evil." But, as I saw nothing bad or did not understand
it if I saw it, I obeyed her reluctantly, without inward conviction and even with a feeling of injury. My aunt, on the
other hand, and her own maids gave quite a different account: They said that my mother was naturally inclined to
be discontented with everything; that she disliked everything about country life and that her bad health was due to
this cause; that, because she was not cheerful herself, she
wished no one else to be cheerful either. These words made
a secret impression on my young mind, the consequence
being that my aunt induced me to go for once without leave
and look on at the acting. This was the way in which it was
arranged. From Christmas till Twelfth Night, my mother
was either not very well or not in good spirits; instead of
reading to us all, my father read to her, merely to send her
to sleep, some book she did not care for or knew already;
after tea, which was always served at six o'clock in the evening, she slept for two hours or more; and during this time
I used to go to my aunt's room. It was on one of these con-
venient occasions that she persuaded me to come and see the
mummers. She wrapped me up, head and all, in a fur coat,
put me in the strong arms of her maid, Matrona, and went
off with me to the carpenter's cottage, where all the maids
and girls of the village were waiting for us, dressed up as
bears or turkeys or cranes, old men or old women. In spite
of the evil smell of tallow candle-ends, the dim light which
a smoky pine torch threw round the large room, and the

stifling atmosphere, how much real merriment there was in these simple revels! Those Christmas songs, surviving from remote antiquity and telling of a vanished world, still preserved their living power to charm and captivate the hearts of the people through countless generations. All present were filled with a kind of intoxication of merriment. Both songs and speeches were constantly drowned by bursts of ringing, hearty laughter. Those were not actors and actresses representing a part for the amusement of others— the dancers and singers expressed their own feelings, and danced and sang to please themselves out of the abundance of their hearts, and each excited spectator was an actor too. The singing and dancing, talking and laughing, were universal; but just when the fun was most fast and furious, the same strong pair of arms wrapped me up in the fur coat and carried me quickly away from that magical fabulous world. On those nights I lay long awake, and strange forms long danced and sang round my bed and kept company with me even in my dreams.

On the first occasion, I was drawn into this act of deception suddenly and almost forcibly; and after I went back to the house, it was long before I could look my mother in the face; but the fascination of the sight had taken such hold of me that I readily agreed to go a second time, and afterwards took the first step myself, begging my aunt that I might go and see the mummers.

At last the severity of the winter came to an end, and the frost became less intense. As we had no thermometers in those days, I cannot say how many degrees of cold we reckoned, but I remember that birds were frozen, and some bodies of sparrows and jackdaws were brought to me, which had fallen dead in flight and turned stiff in a moment; in some cases they were revived by warmth. In general, I ought to remark that the winters of my childhood and early youth were much more severe than they are now; and this is not merely an old man's prejudice, for during my residence at Kazan before the beginning of the year 1807, mercury was twice frozen, so that we could hammer it like hot iron. But this has become a mere legend of the past now at Kazan.

The sun began to give some warmth, and the roads to glitter in his rays. Shrovetide came and brought tobogganing with it. To my regret, my mother would not let me toboggan with the village children. As I coasted down with my sister and sometimes with my little brother, I cast envious glances, as we ran past, at the crowd of village boys and girls, all ruddy with the air and exercise, who sped boldly down all the way from the stackyard at the top of the hill on their small sleds or toboggans or skates. For toboggans, they were content with old sieves or round wicker baskets, shod with ice. The merry, active children, often dressed up in strange costumes, talked and laughed their loudest, especially when a skater flew head over heels, or a toboggan spun quickly round and upset, and the girl-passenger began to shriek long before the shipwreck of her vehicle. How I longed to join in their merry noise and laughter, and after seeing them, how tiresome it seemed to me to toboggan in solitude on the little ice-run which had been made in the garden, in front of the drawing room windows! But I had one consolation, that my sister used to go there with me.

When Lent began, our winter sports, of which we had not many, all came to an end. It cannot be said that Lent in our house was spent in prayer and fasting. My mother did not observe fasts, on the ground of health; I certainly did no fasting; and as to my father, though he ate no meat during Lent and the Fast of the Assumption (August 1 to 15), yet his dinner was much more dainty then than at other times,

owing to the abundant supply of frozen sterlets and stur-
geon from the Ural district, fresh caviar, and burbot from
the tanks. In those days the nearest church was nine versts
away in the village of Mordovsky Buguruslan. For some
reason the priest was not well disposed to us, and we went
there only for the great festivals. In general, it must be said,
our family was not indifferent to religious ordinances, but
the distance of the church had the usual effect, and we were
not accustomed to attend divine service. Thus I spent the
season of Lent in working as usual, or rather harder than
usual, at my books. My own pupil was no longer a cause of
vexation, but gave me pleasure by her progress. With her I
made buildings out of bricks or played with dolls, and sometimes I read fables for children and explained them to her.

During all this time, my mother had something on her
mind and was at times obviously unhappy; and she was
with me less, so that I had more time for quiet reflection.
School life had given a shock to the sweet security of childhood, and my return home had not obliterated the new
impressions. I found that I had lost the old freedom from
care and the old passion for outdoor amusements; I began
to pay more attention to what went on around me and to
understand some things which I had never before noticed.
The radiance of some objects began to fade for me, and a
peculiar feeling of sadness, such as I had never experienced
before, began to cast a shadow over all the amusements and
occupations I had loved so well. This is a sad subject, and
I do not intend to dwell upon it; but some allusion to it is
necessary, in order to explain why life at Aksakovo ceased
after some months to be to me the bright paradise it had
been once, and why I no longer dreaded returning to school;
besides, I was not to go there as a Government scholar.

Winter was long and obstinate, and spring slow in asserting her rights. April was ending, before a warm air, together with wind and rain, attacked the terrible snowdrifts in earnest and routed them in the course of a single week. At Easter the roads were utterly impassable, and we could not even attend the morning service on the great festival. Easter Week brought little happiness to me, for my mother was unwell and depressed, and my father, unusually silent, was constantly poring over documents in connection with a lawsuit against the Bogdanovs about some land; in the end, he won his case. He went every day to the mill, to observe the rise of the water.

One day he came home unexpectedly soon and said to me, "We intend to let the water out of the pond at once, Seryozha; ask your mother if you may come." Off I ran to ask leave, and I was more fortunate than usual, for my mother let me go, after she had taken some precautions against wet feet and chills. We drove to the mill on a long country car and found the laborers waiting for us on the milldam, armed with implements of different kinds. All Russians love to watch moving water, and the population of Aksakovo had collected in a body to watch the process of emptying the pond. A millrace with a sliding gate to exclude the water was unknown in our country in those days, and the opening made in the dam to let out the flood water was filled up again and rammed tight every year. The ice on the pond was swollen and dark and uneven; it had cracked and broken away from the sides, and hardly any water found its way to the machinery. Axes, crowbars, and iron shovels set to work to hack away the frozen dam along the edges of the hole made the year before; the men had hardly cleared away the surface to a depth of two feet when the water began to flow and went to work so effectively, with no further help from man, that in half an hour it had cleared a path for itself. The muddy waves rushed forward impetuously and turned instantly into a powerful river which refused to confine itself to the new channel and inundated the surrounding land. The people saluted with shouts of joy the element they loved as it tore its way to freedom from its winter prison; the shrill voices of the women rose above the rest; and their cries, the splashing of the water as it fell from a height, and the cracking of the ice as it settled down and broke—all this presented a picture full of life. Had not a message come from the house that it was long past dinnertime, my father and I would probably have stayed till the evening to watch it.

Next morning we went back to the dam and found a different scene there, though the noise and merriment were as great as before. The violence of the water's first onset had calmed down a good deal; the level of the pond had fallen noticeably; small blocks of ice had broken against the posts and been swept along, while large blocks had settled at the bottom of the pond where it was shallow. The ground outside the hole in the dam had formerly been almost dry, though a great volume of water was running there now, and short stout stakes had been driven in here before the flood came down. Now the men were wading waist-deep into the water to tie or hang upon the stakes traps of different kinds; the fish driven downstream by the pressure of the water and, still more, the fish that made their way upstream as far as the opening in the dam till they were beaten back by the might of the falling waves, got caught in the traps set for them. The men were dripping wet and shivering with cold, yet they bandied jests and loud cries with one another, as they kept drawing out their spoil upon the bank; and the women and old people and children carried it home, using baskets and sieves for the purpose, or sometimes merely their petticoats. We picked out some large fish and started homewards. My mother was vexed with us for staying so long, and it was some time before I got leave to visit the mill again.

Before long all traces of winter had disappeared; the bushes and trees were clothed with green, the young grass grew up, and spring appeared in all its beauty. As before, our garden was soon populous with songbirds of all kinds which had a special fancy for the old gooseberry bushes and barberries; again the nightingales began to sing, and the mockingbirds to imitate their song. The previous spring I had spent in close confinement, in a narrow room in the hospital, and it would have been natural for me to feel a special pleasure in the contrast; but I had a constant heartache, and though I did not clearly understand the cause of it, yet all my occupations, to which I seemed to devote myself as usual, were poisoned by a feeling of sorrow.

While it was yet winter, my father determined to make a new outlet for the milldam, provided with a sluice, and to build a better mill. For this purpose he employed a miller called Krasnov, a great talker, who turned out eventually to be a great imposter. During the whole of Lent, our laborers were preparing timber of all kinds—large and small beams, joists, planks, and posts; it seemed that all these were required in large numbers. As soon as the floodwater had run down, they began to pierce the dam and build a new channel for the water in a different place. At the same time, hired laborers began to drive piles and then to build a large mill, also in a new position, which was intended to hold six pairs of grinding-stones; there was also to be a crushing-machine in a building of its own. The work went on nearly all summer. My father had a blind belief in Krasnov, but the old miller, Boltunyonok, and some of our peasants, who knew something about the building of mills, grinned and shook their heads when they were by themselves. When my father said, "What do you think of Krasnov? How well he understands his job! He has made a plan of it all on paper; he trusts to his eye in making the piles, and they all fit perfectly!"—our men always answered with the innocent cunning of the Russian peasant: "Oh, he's all alive, *batyushka*, and a capital hand at his job. He works it all out in his head, and everything fits into its place just as it ought to fit. Only one can't tell how the mill is going to work; the water may run slow along that channel, slower than it did when it came straight from the current. We only hope it won't freeze in winter." Krasnov smiled at these criticisms and refuted them with such perfect assurance that it never entered my father's head for a moment to doubt of success. I too listened with reverence and awe to the eloquence of Krasnov.

Meanwhile the building operations made it necessary to let the water out of the pond, and such fishing followed as was never known either before or since. All the fish in the pond made for the river that fed it, and the fish were as thick as they are in a tureen of good fish soup. The number caught was fabulous. I and my attendant Yevseich never left the place and never cast a line anywhere else. My father also, who very seldom had time for it, could fish now from morning till night, because he had to spend most of the day by the mill, watching the building operations; so it was quite easy for him, while fishing, to keep an eye on all the works and examine them from time to time. Chub, carp, perch, pike, and large roach (three or four pounds weight) took constantly and at all hours. The size of the fish depended

on the size of the bait: a large bait always secured a large
fish. My father liked especially to catch perch and pike, and
I remember that he sometimes tied two hooks on one line
and used small fish as bait; and he often had two perch on
at once, and once a perch and a pike. The pike were generally caught in traps which were baited with fair-sized perch;
and some of these pike weighed nearly twenty pounds. We
were not scientific anglers and had no landing nets, so in
spite of thick lines and strong hooks, it is not surprising that
the largest fish often broke our rods or tackle and made off.
Yevseich, whose excitement over fishing even in his old age
often made me laugh, suffered more than anyone from this
cause; thanks to him, I also often lost a large fish, because
I could not pull it out without his help, and his help was in
most cases a hindrance. By the middle of July the best of
the sport was over, and the chub and other large fish ceased
to take. But the smaller fish still gave excellent sport, and
the others would probably have gone on taking, if we had
known then to use whole crayfish as bait.

Throughout this year, my mother corresponded regularly once a month with Upadishevsky. During the twelve-
month a number of changes had taken place in the grammar
school at Kazan. The Rector had retired, and his duties
were now performed by the senior teacher of Russian History, Ilya Yakovkin; Kamashev also had retired, and the
new Head Master was Upadishevsky. Our old friend had
discussed the matter with the new Rector and with the inspector, and now informed us that I might, if my parents
approved, be removed from the list of Government scholars
and enter as a pensioner. This would enable me to live with
one of the teachers; he told us that there were two excellent young men, Ivan Zapolsky and Grigori Kartashevsky,

both graduates of Moscow University, who rented a large house for their common use and took boarders, whom they made exceedingly comfortable at a moderate charge. This news, and especially the disappearance of Kamashev, gave much pleasure to my parents, and though it was a serious burden on them to pay three hundred rubles a year for me and to spend two hundred more on my clothes and books and attendant, they resolved to run into debt for the sake of my education. They owed already 2,500 rubles—in those days even so small a sum was considered "debt," and they would not have ventured to borrow more, but for their expectations from my father's aunt, Praskovya Ivanovna. The school term began on the fifteenth of August, but boys were entered a fortnight earlier. So it was settled that we should start for Kazan at the end of July. I accepted this decision calmly enough, because the secret burden upon my mind had become heavier and more painful. But when our preparations were completed and the day of departure fixed, I began to grieve so at leaving Aksakovo that everything about it suddenly recovered in my eyes all, or more than all, its old preciousness and charm. Feeling that I should never see it again, I said good-bye to every building and every spot, every tree and bush, and I said good-bye with tears. I distributed all my wealth: My pigeons I gave over to our cook Stepan and his son; of my cat I made a present to Sergevnya the wife of our blind man of business, Pantelyei Grigorich, a capital hand at all business and learned in the law; my fishing tackle and traps I divided among the village boys; while my books, dried flowers, pictures, and so on became the property of my sister—between us there had grown up during this year as close a friendship as can exist between a girl of nine and her brother of eleven. To part from her was a great grief to me, and I begged my mother to take her with us. My mother refused at first, but gave way at last to my eager wish.

I ought to mention that the new mill was set going a week before we went away. Alas! the doubts of Boltunyonok and his mates were justified. As they had prophesied, the current was weaker than before, and the six pairs of stones were too much for it; even when a single pair was used, the mill worked much worse than the old one. My father could believe no longer in Kranov's skill; he turned the man out, and charged the old miller to mend matters as best he could.

At last, on the 26th of July, the same roomy carriage as before, with the same coachman and postilion and drawn by the same six horses, was standing by the front steps, and the same crowd of indoor and outdoor servants collected to see us off. My father and mother, with my sister and me and Parasha, took their places in the coach; Yevseich took his seat on the box and Theodore on the rumble; and we started slowly from the house, leaving behind us on the steps my aunt Tatyana, my brother with his nurse, and my youngest sister in the arms of her nurse. Our road went for some distance along the pond, over which flocks of white and pied seagulls were already flitting. How I envied each village boy! *He* was not obliged to go off anywhere or to part with any person or thing; he was staying at home, with full power to sit where he liked on the dam with his fishing rod and angle for perch and roach under the close shade of the alders, with never a care in his head. He was left in undisturbed and undisputed possession of the pond, which, because it had been emptied so late in spring, was free this year from the growth of weed and rushes. For want of exercise, our horses were hot and restless, but the strong and practiced arms of the coachman controlled them and forced them to keep to a walk for a long time. Inside the carriage, we all seemed sad, and no one spoke. I pushed my head out of the window and watched my dear Aksakovo until it disappeared from my sight; and silent tears flowed down my cheeks.

3

꙳

My Return to School

On our arrival at Kazan in the summer of 1801, instead of staying as before with Mme. Aristov, we took somewhat better lodgings. I forget the name of the street, but I remember that we occupied the whole of a small detached house which belonged, I think, to a M. Chortov. Upadishevsky came at once to see us, and this friend and benefactor was greeted by us all as a near kinsman. He told us that Yakovkin was still performing the duties of Rector, but that reports were going about the town to the effect that M. Likhachov, a rich landowner of the district, would soon be appointed to the post. This was a good opportunity, he said, to enter me as a pensioner at the school; for, though Yakovkin and all the Governors had given their consent the future Rector might take a different view of the matter and prove obstinate. Upadishevsky was warm in his praise of two of the senior teachers, Ivan Zapolsky and Grigori Kartashevsky;*

---

* Kartashevsky and Aksakov, the tutor and the pupil, both married in 1816 within one month of each other. Kartashevsky's bride was Nadyezhda Aksakov, the sister of whom the author speaks so often and with such affection. Kartashevsky died in 1840 at Petersburg.

the first taught Physics and the second Pure Mathematics, and both had come to the school some time before from Moscow University. He spoke highly of their intelligence, learning, and regular habits. The two were friends and lived together in a fine stone house, where they took seven boarders, all pensioners at the school; the board and lodging was very good, and much attention was paid to the boys' progress in their school work. It was not their intention to take more boarders, but Upadishevsky had told them about me, and had given such a glowing account of the whole family that the young men, unable to resist his entreaties, had agreed to make an exception in my mother's favor and to include me among their pupils.

My father took me to call on the acting Rector and got permission for me to enter as a pensioner; we next called on the two young masters and met with a friendly reception in each place. Kartashevsky explained that they divided the pupils between them and that the three oldest boys, who were under his immediate supervision, would complete the school course within the year and go away to enter the Civil Service. As it was his intention to set up house for himself after that and take no more pupils, he said that I ought to apply to his friend and colleague, Zapolsky. To my father it was all one, which of them took me; but he pressed both the young men to come and make the acquaintance of my mother. They came next day, and my mother, as soon as she saw him, formed a very favorable impression of Kartashevsky, and much regretted that I was not to be under him. But my father and I much preferred Zapolsky: he seemed to us more cordial and friendly and sociable than his solemn colleague. All my mother's friendly expostulations—that the two friends, instead of parting, ought to live together and help one another in the performance of such sacred duties, were ineffectual. Kartashevsky replied very firmly that he found this duty too serious and too absorbing; that to be responsible for the education of young people was a burden he could not discharge to his own satisfaction, even if the parents were satisfied; and that his study of science, in which he was still a learner, was hindered by such ties. His reply was so positive that any attempt to continue the discussion would have been useless and awkward as well. When the two young men left us, my mother expressed her disappointment with her usual vivacity. She was always too much carried away by her instinctive feelings, and now she praised to the skies the merits of Kartashevsky, while she found many defects in his colleague. The sequel proved that my mother's eager enthusiasm was not at fault. For though Zapolsky was quite a "good" man, in the ordinary sense of that word, the other belonged to a select class among mankind—those who have an exceptionally high standard of duty and spend all their lives in rigid observation of that standard. But I was delighted to think that the good-natured Zapolsky was to be my tutor and that I was to live, not with the big boys who had quarters of their own, but with my equals in age, lively and good-natured boys like myself. Thanks to the interest taken by Upadishevsky, all our business was settled without difficulties of any kind, and within a month my parents and my sister went back to Aksakovo. But during this month Kartashevsky, though he passed for a confirmed recluse, paid us many visits; he could appreciate my mother, and a lasting friendship was formed between them, a friendship founded on mutual respect and tested in the course of time by many events of importance.

This second parting from my mother did not cost me anything like the pain and misery that had accompanied our former separation. I noticed the difference in myself especially, and young as I was, I was impressed by it and had some regretful thoughts. But before long the new life absorbed all my attention. I occupied a room with three brothers named Manasein, and we became good friends at once; a small room near ours was occupied by a single tenant, a boy called A. He was very rich, and I think he was the only son of his mother, a widow. In spite of his wealth, which was obvious from his clothes and bedding and all his belongings, he was not at all generous. He kept a large iron-bound chest in his room and always carried the key in his pocket. This chest excited general curiosity, and my schoolfellows believed that its contents were very valuable and precious.

At last I set eyes again on the school buildings that I had once feared and hated, and I was much pleased to find that the sight did not produce in me either fear or any unpleasant feeling. I was placed in the Junior Class as before. Most of my former companions had been promoted to the Middle Form, and their places were filled by new boys, less well prepared than I had been, while those who had failed to get their remove were either idle or stupid. Hence in a very short time I was top of the form in all subjects except in the Catechism and *Outlines of Sacred History*. The priest continued to keep up a sort of ill will against me, though I always knew my lessons for him very accurately. This fact seems worth noting: Upadishevsky asked him later why Aksakov, who worked very hard at other subjects, was not at the top with him, and added, "I suppose he does not know his lessons." "No," said the priest, "his work is very well done, but he has no liking for the Catechism and Sacred History."

The course of a few months dispersed the last traces of homesickness and longing for the freedom of the country; by degrees I became accustomed to school life, made some real friends among the boys, and became fond of the school.

This change of feeling was largely due to the fact that I did not live in the school and only went there for lessons. Life in my tutor's house was not so entirely unlike my life at home as my former condition had been, when I was shut up permanently in a Government institution and surrounded by a number of companions of all classes.

At first A. avoided intercourse with me and the Manaseins, and indeed with all the boys, but when he noticed how quiet and peaceable I was, he began to talk to me and invite me to his room; he went so far as to treat me to some of the delicacies from home which he generally devoured in secrecy. At last he offered to show me his chest, but it must, he said, be done in such a way that no one else should know of it. My imagination, full of fairy tales, pictured this receptacle as filled with precious stones or ingots of gold and silver, and I was delighted. It was arranged that I should come to his room when all were asleep, and I did so that same evening. The Manaseins did not keep me waiting long, for they soon began to snore; off I went to A.'s room, where there was always a lamp burning at night before a large sacred picture in a rich gilt frame. When he had lit a candle and locked the door, he made me promise to tell no one of what I was about to see and then carefully unlocked the mysterious chest. But a great surprise awaited me. It turned out that the chest was packed full of inferior pictures! There were engravings and drawings, landscapes and portraits in oil, the latter like the signs displayed over barbers' shops. Though I was a lover of pictures myself, I paid no attention to them now, because I was expecting something entirely different, and I was hoping all the time that the real treasure would be revealed at the bottom of the chest; so, when the last sheets had been taken out and the bare boards met my eyes, I could not help calling out, "Is that all!" This was a terrible disappointment to A., who expected me to be surprised and delighted. Talking in a whisper, I frankly confessed the belief that we all entertained about his chest. "You are a pack of fools," said A. angrily, and he almost turned me out of the room; and that was the end of our boyish friendship. Some time later, I broke my promise and disclosed the contents of the chest to the Manasein boys, and we looked several times through the chinks in the locked door and watched A., while he spread out his pictures on the bed and tables and chairs and even on the floor. He looked at them, dusted them, and admired them, as Pushkin's *Avaricious Knight* gloated over his treasures; he gave himself up to this pleasure almost every night for whole hours. We began to make fun of him and spread in the school the story of his passion for pictures; and soon he was pestered by mischievous boys who called upon him to share his riches with others, and to let them see "The Mice Burying the Cat," or "Yeruslan Defeating a Horde of Unbelievers." A. abused them in his wrath and even used his fists, but nothing would stop them. At last he became so weary of this that he wrote to his mother, and she soon took him away from the school for good. Of course, there may have been other reasons as well for his removal. Not long ago I heard that A. was very eccentric in later life also; but that does not prevent him from enjoying a high reputation for the practical management of his land.

During the first few months after my entrance, Zapolsky gave a certain amount of attention to me and his other pupils. He asked us beforehand about the lessons set for us to learn, and he taught us some French and German; and that was all. But he gradually ceased to pay us any attention at all and began to absent himself, though we did not know where he went. To tell the truth, our studies profited by his absences, because Kartashevsky took us in hand at such times, and he taught us, as I could see very well, much more carefully and much better than his colleague. At last Yevseich told me in confidence that Zapolsky was courting a young lady of good family and possessed of some means; that she herself and her mother were favorable to his views; but her father was unwilling to give her hand to a teacher who had no money and was also the son of a priest. This information turned out to be quite accurate.

As was expected, M. Likhachov was appointed Rector, but the boys in boarding houses did not even know him by sight for a long time, because he commonly visited the school at the dinner hour and never even looked into the classrooms. I learned my lessons and drove or walked to the school very cheerfully. I do not know whether my present companions were different or if the difference was in myself—anyhow, I felt nothing of the teasing and bullying that I had found so unbearable before; I found common interests with others, and a desire sprang up within me for social intercourse with them, so that I began to look forward impatiently to school hours. I ought to add that most of my time at the school was spent in form, where my vanity was constantly flattered by the approval of the teachers and a certain measure of respect on the part of my schoolfellows; but this last did not prevent me from joining their noisy games during all our free time and on every suitable occasion. I wrote home every week, and every week I received very affectionate letters from my mother, to which my father sometimes added a postscript. My mother assured me that she was not grieving over our separation and that she was glad to get from Zapolsky and Upadishevsky such good accounts of my conduct and diligence. When she said that she was not grieving, I believed her. In every letter she sent her kind regards to Zapolsky and Kartashevsky, and from time to time corresponded with them herself. And so things went on for nearly a year—till June of 1802. The examinations took place in June, and they resulted in a complete triumph for my youthful vanity! I was promoted to the Middle Form in all subjects. At our Speech Day, which was at the beginning of July, I received a prize with a gilt inscription on the boards, "For diligence and proficiency"; I also got a Certificate of Merit.

A plain, covered cart and three horses with a coachman had been sent for me from home some time before; and after dinner on Speech Day I set off with Yevseich for our dear Aksakovo. We traveled along the same road as two years before, when my mother carried me off in triumph from my prison, and we halted at the same places for food and sleep. The breath of nature soon penetrated my being, driving out of my head all thoughts of school, of boys and masters, books and lessons. After a period of apparent forgetfulness or indifference, I fell in love with the beauties of God's world more fervently than ever and more consciously. At home, all my family greeted me with tender love, and my mother's happiness it is impossible to describe. My sister had grown much taller and much prettier in the course of the year, and she was delighted to see her brother again. How many questions there were to ask, how many stories to tell! She told me for one thing that my mother had made herself quite ill by her grief at parting from me; and I felt a kind of pain to think that I had suffered so little this time from the separation.

All the days I spent at Aksakovo during these holidays melt in my memory into one happy day of splendid weather; I could not, if I wished, tell what I did—I only know that I enjoyed myself from morning till night. In the swarm of my pleasures, fishing, bathing, and hawking are the most prominent. My mother made me repeat every trifling detail of my life at school during the year, and as I went on, she said again and again to my father, "You see, Alexei Stepanich, I was not mistaken about Kartashevsky. He is as far above Zapolsky as the sky above the earth; he is the man whom I should like to have for Seryozha's tutor, and I shall use every effort to bring that about." She was confirmed in this purpose by what Yevseich told her, and I myself understood the importance of the change and wished it to be made. My mother was attracted chiefly by the high standards and strict principles of Kartashevsky.

From my sister I hardly ever parted at this time; our friendship became even closer and more tender. But the happy days flew by on wings, and on the 10th of August, the same covered cart with the same horses and the same coachman carried me off with Yevseich on our way to Kazan.

On my arrival I found all the boys had returned. But Zapolsky was absent, and we were told that he had gone off to be married to Nastasya Yelagin, the young lady whom he had been courting. After their honeymoon, the young pair would come to Kazan and receive us in a house of their own which they intended to take; Kartashevsky would look after us till then. I was delighted by this prospect, but the Manasein boys were not, especially the youngest brother, Elpidifor, a fine boy but very mischievous and idle then, though the mischievous boy grew up to be an active and useful man.

I remember very well the eager anxiety to learn with which I entered the Middle Form. I knew beforehand that the lessons there were much more difficult and that this form was considered to be the critical stage of a boy's school career. It was generally believed that a scholar who distinguished himself there was sure to earn distinction also in the Senior Class, whereas it often happened that the top boys in the Junior Class never did very much in the Middle Form.* This belief alarmed me, and my fears were not dispelled during the whole of the first month. The teachers were different, and we were strangers to them. The boys who had been promoted sat all by themselves on two separate benches, and little attention was paid to them at first by the teachers. Owing to the difficulty of the work, most boys spent two years in this form; hence the classes were so large that it was physically impossible for the teacher to give equal attention to us all. One of the subjects taught in this form was Slavonic Grammar together with Russian; the textbook we used was written by our teacher of the subject, Nikolai Ibrahimov, a graduate of Moscow University. He taught Russian literature and mathematics in the same form. His surname and his appearance alike clearly betrayed his Tartar or Bashkir origin; his head was large, his eyes small and piercing, with a very pleasant expression; he had prominent cheekbones and a huge mouth. This man had a great influence on my literary development, and his memory is dear to me. He first encouraged me and gave me what I may call a push in the right direction. He used to dictate from his *Slavonic Grammar*, for the benefit of those who had not heard the work explained or did not possess a copy of it. The custom was for one pupil to write on the board at his dictation while the rest copied down what was dictated. Ibrahimov's explanations were not sufficiently detailed and not quite clear; his comments, though they did well enough for those who were going through the grammar a second

* It is obvious that three forms were too few. When this was proved by experience, grammar schools were divided into seven classes. (Author's note)

time, were not enough for the new boys and especially for those who, like myself and many others, were only twelve years old. But fortunately, owing to Zapolsky's absence, Kartashevsky was supervising my preparation at this time, and he explained to me the *Introduction to Slavonic Grammar*, which contained a view of grammar in general. Without his explanations I should have understood as little of this *Introduction* as the other boys did. I possessed already a complete manuscript copy of the *Slavonic Grammar*, and I read this through on Sundays, asking my tutor to explain points that were dark to me; and this practice proved of no small service to me afterwards.

At the end of September, six weeks after the term had begun, Ibrahimov changed his method. The little Tartar figure, after walking once or twice along the whole row, book in hand, instead of dictating as usual, suddenly drew near to the benches where the new boys sat by themselves. My heart began to beat hard. He first put questions to all the boys who had been promoted from the lower form, taking the questions from the Introduction and first two chapters of the *Grammar* which we had already gone through, and examining us according to the order in which we sat. The order was as follows; first came the Government scholars, then the exhibitioners, and lastly the pensioners. Questions upon the *Grammar* were fairly well answered; but of the *Introduction* no one knew anything at all—a clear proof that they did not understand it. At last my turn came. I answered questions on the *Grammar* readily and satisfactorily, and Ibrahimov said, "Good!" after each answer. He began to get interested, and asked me twenty questions instead of the usual three or four, and I answered them all with equal success. The big Tartar mouth stretched its widest, as Ibrahimov smiled again and again; at last he said,

"Very good indeed! Now let us see what you can make of the *Introduction*." My answers were no less satisfactory than before. Then he tried to puzzle me but failed, because I really understood the subject and was not merely repeating words that I had learned by rote. Ibrahimov was surprised and delighted beyond measure. He showered compliments upon me; then he made me stand up and collect all my class books, and led me by the hand to the top desk. "That is your place," he said, and made me sit third in a class of more than forty boys. Such a triumph I had never even dreamed of, and I was perfectly happy. On returning home, I sent Yevseich to ask Kartashevsky if I might come to his room; and when leave was granted, I told him with great joy what had happened to me. Though he was in reality much pleased both by my success and the spirit in which I took it, yet he answered dryly enough, as his system required: "Don't be too happy over it; possibly Ibrahimov was in too much of a hurry. You are bound now to work still harder and confirm his good opinion." Such an answer might have discouraged or repelled many boys—and I decidedly disapprove of such a method myself—but I understood Kartashevsky already. Before this he had praised me highly in letters to my mother without letting me see that he was pleased with me; he even asked her not to show me his letters.

Russian Literature was another subject taught by Ibrahimov, and my success in this was no less pronounced. He taught the syntax of the Russian language and made us write exercises, consisting partly in dictation and partly in turning passages of verse into prose. The dictation was very good for us, not only as practice in writing, but because it helped to form our taste, for Ibrahimov used to choose the best passages from Karamzin, Dmitriev, Lomonosov, and Kheraskov, which he made us read aloud, and then explained their literary merit. To paraphrase of verse he did not himself attach much value and only made us do it occasionally, merely because it was one of the prescribed subjects. He preferred to give us practice in the writing of short compositions upon subjects which he set himself. As to other subjects—in general history, Russian history, and geography, which we did with Yakovkin, I did well, but was not of the best. In languages generally, the standard attained was not high, and this was certainly due to bad teaching. In arithmetic, I was weak even in the Junior Class; in the Middle Form it became clear that I was quite unable to learn mathematics, and this reputation I kept at the University as well as at school. In writing, drawing, and dancing, I got on well enough. In my lessons with the priest I did well, but not very well. While in this form I ceased to use a slate, which was then, and still is to some extent, a pet aversion with me: the squeaking of a slate pencil upon a slate grates on my nerves now as it used to do then.

At last we heard that Zapolsky had brought his bride back to Kazan and was staying at his mother-in-law's house. He came next day to see his pupils and was exceedingly cordial to us. Yevseich told me in confidence that Kartashevsky was very angry with his colleague for prolonging his absence from one month to three and said, "I am quite tired of bothering about these brats, but I cannot leave them as you do without supervision and attention." Zapolsky apologized, thanked him for what he had done, and tried to embrace him, but his friend treated him very sternly and roughly, threatening to leave the house and give up the care of the boys unless the young pair set up an establishment of their own without delay. I should add that Kartashevsky had now ceased to have any pupils of his own. In spite of these threats, it was some time before Zapolsky took any lodgings, and Kartashevsky lived on in our house two months longer, attending steadily and scrupulously to our comfort and conduct and supervising our studies. During these five months I became much attached to him, though he never once spoke affectionately to me and never dropped the appearance of dryness and severity. I was too young to appreciate his real worth, and I could not have got to care for him if my mother had not secretly informed me that he really loved me and praised me highly, though he concealed his feelings, fearing that his praise might be injurious to so young a boy. Kartashevsky in his long and useful career held important posts where he had to associate not with children only but with men advanced in years; yet he never abandoned this mistaken principle, and the result was unfortunate. Those whom circumstances enabled to know him intimately kept through life a deep respect and devotion to him; but on the other hand, many good people were repelled by the well-meant dryness of his manner, and believed him, quite unjustly, to be proud and unfeeling.

Zapolsky did at last take suitable lodgings, and we all went to live there. I shed tears on parting with Kartashevsky and would have embraced him; but he would not allow it, and, though I found out later from a letter he wrote to my mother that he was very near weeping himself, he said dryly and coldly, "What is all this about? What are you crying for? I suppose you are afraid that Zapolsky will be stricter with you." I admit that I was hurt by such words at such a moment.

I forgot to say that Zapolsky brought his bride to see us; all we noticed was that she had no eyebrows and never stopped blushing; and she was so simple that she was unable to say a word of greeting to the boys. In the new house, the Manasein boys and I occupied a wing by ourselves. We were left entirely to our own devices, and now I realized the wide difference between our new tutor and his predecessor. The former we never saw except at dinner and supper: the young husband was completely taken up either with the arrangements required by his change of condition or with the management of a small property of sixty serfs that had come to him as his wife's dowry. The property was twenty versts from Kazan, and he went there for two days every week. The rest of his time was spent in teaching physics to the Senior Class or in attending to his wife's family; three of her sisters were grown-up, and they were regular inmates of his household. Yet no one attended to the management of the house, and it was very badly done. Even our food was wretched, and thus I got involved in a scrape which I must describe.

We always had supper in the large house at a common table, and one evening there was ham for supper. I cut off a piece and was just going to put it into my mouth when Yevseich, who was standing in back of my chair, nudged me from behind. I turned round and stared at him in surprise; he shook his head and winked at me, meaning that I was not to eat the ham. So I laid the piece of ham down on the plate and noticed for the first time that the meat was bad, actually crawling; I gave up my plate as quickly as I could. I was sitting quite close to Zapolsky, and he saw all that had happened. I should add that his wife, with her mother and three sisters, was sitting at table, as well as the boys. When supper was over and we all went to Zapolsky to say goodnight before going to bed, he told me to stay, and took me and Yevseich off to his study. There he rebuked me with great severity for impertinent behavior; he said that, on purpose to disgrace him, I had directed the attention of all the party to the spoiled ham, though everyone else had eaten it out of politeness. After reading me a long lecture and proving that I had committed an unpardonable crime, he next abused my worthy Yevseich in most insulting terms. Not understanding in the least how I was to blame, I began to cry, from a sense of undeserved insult. This softened Zapolsky's heart; he said that he forgave me; he even wished to embrace me, but I said very frankly that I was not crying because I was sorry for what I had done, but because he had wronged me by suspecting me unjustly of a bad intention, and because he had abused Yevseich. He got very angry again. He actually said that I was a hardened sinner and should suffer exemplary punishment the next day. Then he let me go to bed.

But it was long before I fell asleep: the thought that a comparative stranger intended to inflict severe punishment on me, for no fault of mine, wounded and irritated my feelings excessively. Never within my recollection had anyone laid a hand upon me, except my mother; and even that was an old story. At last I fell asleep. Next morning we dressed and went across to the house for our tea. Zapolsky, contrary to custom, joined us there, and explained my crime to the Manasein boys and Yelagin, his brother-in-law, who had joined the school a fortnight before. Then they were sent off to school, but I was sentenced to be deprived of tea, and kept out of school. I was to go back to our wing, undress, and go to bed, and there I was to stay till evening, with a slice of bread and a glass of water for lunch and dinner. A punishment so silly and so entirely undeserved was bound to seem, and did seem, an unbearable insult to a boy as sensitive and precocious as I was; and I did really feel hardened, as I looked with a contemptuous smile at my tutor and then hurried off to our wing. I undressed and went to bed, taking a book with me for occupation. My faithful Yevseich, though he could not grasp the injury to my feel-

ings and laughed heartily at so absurd a punishment, was
distressed to think that I should not have enough to eat, and
he promised to procure for me on the sly anything tempt-
ing that was served in the dining room. But I angrily for-
bade him to do this, and sent him out of the room. At first I
felt only rage and irritation; then I began to cry, and finally
went to sleep. Owing to my bad night, I slept so soundly
that I never woke till my companions came back to the wing
after dining with the family, and began to make a noise
over their games. Sleep had calmed my feelings; I refused
the bread and water and remained indifferent to the jokes
of the boys at my expense; they agreed with me that I was
innocent, and laughed less at me than at the oddity of my
punishment. The second Manasein boy was a confirmed
idler, and he even envied me, saying that he would welcome
that form of punishment every day. When the others went
off to afternoon school, I began to prepare the work set
that morning in my absence and to go over the work of the
evening before. At seven o'clock, when the boys had come
back from school and were having tea in the dining room,
Zapolsky sent a message to me to dress and join them, and
I obeyed.

He greeted me by saying, "I forgive you; but you owe it
to these ladies that the time of your punishment is short-
ened," and he pointed to his mother-in-law, his wife, and
her sisters. I expressed my thanks to them. Then he and
his wife immediately left the house for some reason, and
the boys, having finished their tea, went off to the wing,
but the ladies kept me. In no time a small table was laid
and food brought in; the young ladies made me sit at the
table and sat round me themselves. They fed me almost out
of their own hands, and even produced a pot of jam, on
which I feasted with a will. These benefits were conferred

with so much kindness that my heart was quite melted. It turned out that, though the young ladies had never spoken a word to me till then, they had long before taken a fancy to me for my modest behavior; and my punishment, which they and their mother thought undeserved and inhuman, had excited their warmest sympathy! Zapolsky had been unable to resist their intercession on my behalf. I was told that Katerina had even shed tears and gone down on her knees before him—which made Katerina blush terribly. They kept me in the house all the evening. As may be guessed, I chattered freely. Not only did I tell them about my dear Aksakovo and my first term at school, but I recited to them a great deal of poetry, having long had a passion for recitation. The young ladies were sincerely delighted; they uttered cries of pleasure and showered caresses upon me. I was delighted too by the impression I had produced, and my head was turned with youthful vanity. After supper I went back to the wing, where the other boys, who knew already from Yelagin how his sisters had fed and comforted me, asked me questions and expressed their envy of my luck. I was kept awake a long time by excitement and vague fancies beyond my comprehension.

This incident seems trifling enough, but I had a purpose in describing it so fully. It made me idle, though I had worked hard till then. Mme. Yelagin as well as her daughters took a fancy to me and often asked permission of her son-in-law to invite me to spend the evening with them, and I found a couple of hours passed in their society very agreeable. On Sundays and holidays I constantly ran across to their house and almost ceased to visit some ladies, relations of my father's, who had often entertained me in the past. The other boys went on envying me, and Yelagin, a young scamp of fifteen whom his sisters would not invite to join us, was seriously vexed with me, and showed it by caustic allusions, of which I entirely missed the point. By degrees my attention was taken off my work altogether. After three months Zapolsky hired a teacher for us, a divinity student who had finished his course; his name was Guri Lastochkin, and he was a very modest and intelligent young man, from whom I might have gained much, but my work was very badly done until spring came and the Yelagins went off to the country. There was one exception: in Russian Literature and Slavonic Grammar, the subjects taught by Ibrahimov, I still distinguished myself because I had a strong liking for the subject and for the teacher. Six weeks before the examinations I began to work in real earnest. Lastochkin gave zealous assistance to my endeavours and took a great liking to me at this time; but in spite of all, I was not promoted to the Senior Class and had to stay where I was for a year longer. Only a third of my form were promoted, and some of these owed their remove not to proficiency but to seniority, after remaining two or three years in the form. No one blamed me for this, and I professed, like all the others, that it would be good for me to stay in the form two years as most boys did; yet my youthful vanity was hurt, and still worse, I feared that my mother would be vexed.

But my fears were groundless. When I went home to Aksakovo with Yevseich for the summer holidays of 1803, and when my mother had read the letters from Upadishevsky, Zapolsky, and Kartashevsky, she and my father were very well pleased that I had not been promoted. But when I told her fully and frankly the way in which I had been passing my time in my tutor's house, she became very serious and looked dissatisfied. She disapproved of Zapolsky and his relations, and even of Lastochkin, for she could not endure divinity students, and here my father, who had a contemptuous nickname for them, agreed with her entirely. This prejudice was especially unfair in the case of Lastoch-kin, who had many good points.

I had a strange meeting with Lastochkin a few years later. I should say that we became very intimate, in spite of the difference of our ages, at the end of that term; he con-fided all his private affairs to me, telling me for one thing that the Government was urging him to enter the sacred profession, though he felt no leaning in that direction. I do not know why, but I felt convinced that he would certainly enter the priesthood, and I told him so. He denied it with some heat, and in order to convince me of the contrary, he took a sheet of paper one day and wrote on it, "Sooner shall the river at Kazan flow upward than Guri Lastochkin take priest's orders." Then he gave me the paper to keep as a guarantee that he would retain his freedom—a clear proof of his own youth at the time. Two months passed, and we parted; then for nearly four years I never once heard of him, and had quite forgotten his existence.

One wretched autumn morning I received a note from my aunt, my mother's half-sister, whom I loved very dearly; she was living then with the B——s, and I often saw her. "My dear Sergei," she wrote, "Come to our house at six this evening, wearing your uniform and sword.* There is a wed-ding in this house; and you, as the bride's page, must put on her shoes and escort her to church." The bride had been brought up by the B——s; she was poor but young and pretty. When I got there, I was scolded for being a little late and taken at once to the bride's room where I put on her silk stockings and shoes. She was not quite dressed, but her head was in proper bridal trim, and I remember that I

* Students carried swords.

was struck by her beauty. I had hardly time to exchange a few words with my aunt in her room, before the lady of the house sent for me and asked me to drive at once in her carriage to the bridegroom's lodgings. I was to tell him that the bride was dressed and that he should go at once to the church and send a message from there that he was waiting. I went off instantly and had no time to ask the bridegroom's name. A friend was with me who knew the bridegroom and where he lived. He took me to a large Government building inhabited by a number of people, led me through several rooms, and then opened a door. "There," he said, "is the bridegroom, dressing in front of the looking glass." I saw the back of a stout man; he was wearing knee breeches, silk stockings, and shoes, and a servant was hastily fitting on to him a stiff white shirt-front. When I came close, the bridegroom turned round—it was Lastochkin, though grown very stout. A cry of surprise burst from each of us. "My dear Aksakov," he said, embracing me, "how glad I am to see you! But at this moment you must excuse me..." I interrupted him by saying that I was the bride's page and had been sent to hurry the bridegroom. He went on dressing in haste, talking to me all the time. "A great surprise to you, I suppose," he said. "Yes," I answered, "I did not know who the bridegroom was; but I congratulate you on marrying a good and pretty girl." "Oh, you are quite in the dark still," said he; then he took me aside and said in a low voice, "You probably remember my declaration in writing not to take orders. Well, tomorrow I shall be a priest, and next day senior curate in the Cathedral of Peter and Paul," and tears came to his eyes. I do know what circumstances altered his convictions; but he evidently regretted the loss of his freedom. We never met again. In the course of fifteen years I often heard that he was universally loved for his qualities of heart and respected for his learning. I think he became Rector of the seminary recently founded at Kazan.

What chiefly troubled my mother about my school life was the absurd punishment inflicted on me by Zapolsky. The wish to take me away from him and place me with his former colleague rose again in her heart with renewed strength. It was not difficult to take me away, but it seemed hopeless to induce Kartashevsky to break through a rule that he had laid down once for all; the difficulty was increased by the fact that he was not merely a colleague of Zapolsky's, but also an intimate friend. The loss of his best pupil might injure Zapolsky's reputation with other parents, and my transference to Kartashevsky might, by people who were ignorant of the circumstances, be called unhandsome. My poor mother was very sad about it, but she saw no way to mend matters.

To my great astonishment, she disapproved also of the notice taken of me by the kind ladies at my boarding house, and especially of the blandishments of one of the sisters. She decided to travel to Kazan in winter; she wished to see my manner of life for herself, and also to urge Kartashevsky by every means in her power to fall in with her plan. She also had a third motive, which I discovered later: she intended that I should spend with her, and not in the bosom of my tutor's family, all my free time during the Christmas holidays.

All my summer holidays I spent in the country, and I was as happy as in the previous year. But on my return to Kazan I fell in with an adventure that made a deep impression on my mind; indeed, the traces of it remain to this day. From it I date an increased fear, which possesses me still, of ferrying across great rivers. It happened in the following way. We came in the afternoon to the bank of the Kama, opposite the village of Shuran; during summer the river was crossed at this point. On the bank were three loaded carts with their drivers, waiting to cross, and about a score of peasant women with baskets full of berries which they were carrying home to the other side. No ferrymen were to be seen; they had all wandered off somewhere. After some discussion the peasants and my servants determined to take us across themselves, for one of the peasants asserted that he had been a ferryman for some years, and offered himself to the steering oar. Accordingly they picked out the best of the ferryboats; the three carts with the horses and my carriage and three horses were all put on board, and of course, all the women with their baskets came too. The man who professed to be a ferryman took his place at the steering oar; the other four oars were taken by two peasants, my coachman, and my servant Ivan, whose courage and great strength made him worth ten ordinary men. Meanwhile a black cloud was rising quickly in the west and gradually covered the horizon; it was impossible to help noticing it, but we all thought that it might pass to one side or that we might get over before it burst. Though the starting point was exactly opposite Shuran, it was necessary to punt upstream for more than a verst, to prevent the boat from being carried down beyond the landing place by the swift current of the angry Kama. This process was very slow, and the storm came quickly nearer and nearer. To save time, we went only half the right distance up the stream; then the men took to their oars again, crossed themselves, and began to row straight across. But before we had reached the middle of the river, the cloud advanced with astonishing speed till it covered the sky from end to end, the heavens grew black and the reflection in the water still blacker, darkness came on, and a frightful storm burst over us with thunder and light-

ning and a hurricane of wind. Our steersman dropped his
oar in a panic, and confessed that he was not a ferryman at
all and could not steer; an eddy whirled our boat round like
a shaving and carried it down the stream; the women raised
a piercing shriek, and horror fell upon us all. I was so frightened that I trembled all over and could not utter a word.
The rapid current carried us down several versts, and then
stranded us on a sandy shoal about a hundred yards from
the far bank. Ivan sprang into the water which was waist-
deep; then he waded ashore, and the water nowhere came
higher than his breast. Next, he came back the same way
to the boat, made the quietest of our horses jump off, and
mounted me on it, bidding me hold on tight to the horse's
neck and mane. Then he led the horse by the bridle, while
Yevseich walked alongside and supported me with both
arms. Great waves of discolored water surged past us and
drenched even our heads. Unluckily, Ivan, who was walking in front, missed the ford he had traversed twice already,
and got into deep water. All in a moment he disappeared
below the surface, my horse began to swim, and Yevseich
was left behind—and the fear of immediate death that came
over me then I have never forgotten. I was ready to faint
and almost choked by the waves; it was fortunate for me
that it grew shallower after a few yards. Ivan was a strong
swimmer, and he swam on to the shallows, never letting go
of the horse's bridle till he brought him safely to the bank.
But Yevseich was nearly drowned; he could not swim well
and had much difficulty in getting to land. I was taken off
the horse almost unconscious and wet to the skin; my fingers
had stiffened as they clung to the mane. But I soon recovered, and was inexpressibly joyful to find myself safe.

Yevseich stayed with me, while Ivan went back to the
boat. The women, crying and shrieking but refusing to part

with their baskets, were jumping into the water; the peasants were pulling off their horses and carts; and at last they hit upon a safer passage and all made their way somehow to the bank through shallow water. The boat, now lightened of most of its freight, rose off the sand and began to drift down. At this point Ivan's great strength did us yeoman's service: he held the boat fast till my coachman had got off both carriage and horses into the water; then he let go, and off went the boat downstream. The two men, up to the waist in water, harnessed the horses and brought the carriage to land. Everything in it was soaked. Wet and cold, we got in and drove fast to Shuran, where we were warmed and dried and drank plenty of hot tea; and our cold bath was followed by no bad consequences. But I had had a terrible fright, and ever since, the sight of a great river, even in calm weather, has made me uneasy, while a storm produces in me an involuntary horror that I cannot overcome.

On returning to school, I set to work in earnest at my lessons, and as the Yelagins were in the country, I had no distractions. Lastochkin was pleased with my diligence and coached me zealously, so that I soon rose high in all subjects except mathematics. Of the work with Ibrahimov I need not speak, for there I was always at the top. By this time I had become strongly attached to the school, the masters, and the boys, in whom I found cheerful companions. I was no longer confused by the constant bustle and running about, the noise of loud voices and loud laughter; I was unconscious of it all and took my part with the best of them, and found something attractive and orderly in the life.

The autumn was long and wet. There was a serious epidemic of fever in the town, and I was one of the sufferers. Dr. Benis had left the school, and our old friend Andrei Ritter attended to all the boys, including those who like myself lived in boarding houses. His treatment soon checked the fever, but it returned in a few days. Large doses of quinine and Glauber's salts, at the thought of which my gorge rises even now, routed the fever a second time, but it returned a fortnight in a severer form, and the illness dragged on for some time. Yevseich, seeing that the remedies were doing little good, began to doubt the skill of the doctor—whom he had known before as a heavy drinker, and who was sometimes "half-seas-over," according to Yevseich, when he came to see me. So my servant ventured to report this to Zapolsky and asked him to call in another doctor. Zapolsky was very angry; saying that Ritter was famous all over the town for his success with fevers, he sent Yevseich about his business. But Yevseich, who was devoted to me, remembered his promise to his mistress and wrote to tell her of my illness. My mother was much distressed and alarmed. She had not recovered from her confinement—our family had just been increased by the birth of a third brother—but she started at once and traveled alone to Kazan, where she took lodgings for herself and me, called in the best doctor, and nursed me herself. This journey was a fresh act of self-sacrifice on my mother's part: her health suffered seriously in consequence; but her whole life was made up of such actions. Some disagreeable explanations with Zapolsky were inevitable. He was offended by my mother's moving me to her lodgings and by her changing the doctor. But while I was recovering, which took some time owing to severe pain in my right side, Zapolsky had some difficulties with the parents of the Manasein boys, which made him give up his boarding house and announce that he would take no more pupils.

This was a great satisfaction to my mother. She would not have left me with Zapolsky in any case, but she would have found it much more difficult or even impossible to induce

Kartashevsky to take me directly from his friend. Even as it was, she met with so many difficulties that success for long seemed doubtful. I ought to say that, during all the second period of my school-time, the friendly relations between Kartashevsky and my family showed no signs of falling off, but grew steadily closer. My mother carried on a very active correspondence with him, and he could not fail to appreciate her intelligence, her steady friendship for him, founded on respect for his high character, and her exceptional devotion to her child. More than once I was within hearing in another room while she urged and entreated Kartashevsky with the fire of heartfelt eloquence and burning tears to take me as his pupil. At last she broke down his opposition and he consented, though very unwillingly. He took me, not as a pupil or boarder, but as a young companion— he was then twenty-seven, and I thirteen. He refused positively to accept money for his charge, and he proposed that we should share the expense of board and lodging, though for the sake of convenience, I was to have my own supply of tea; all our other expenditure each of us was to manage independently. When my mother had at last secured the fulfillment of her darling wish, she was so radiantly happy that I felt deeply how far superior a mother's love is to that of anyone else in the world. I too was very glad to come under Kartashevsky. I felt a profound respect for him, and even loved him. His rather strange and dry manner did not frighten me, for I knew that this cold exterior, due to his views on education, was part of a regular system in his dealings with boys; and I thought then that perhaps it was the right system, though I certainly do not think so now.

A house belonging to the Yelagins, a fairly good and roomy house that was standing empty and on lease at the time, was taken by us at once. My mother moved there with me and made arrangements about our future housekeeping. I was now quite well again, and when she had handed me over personally to the care of Kartashevsky, she went back to the rest of the family at Aksakovo, full of bright hopes for the future. This was in February of the year 1804.

My life with Grigori Kartashevsky is one of the happiest memories of my early youth. It lasted two and a half years; although its brightness suffered some eclipse eventually, yet only the happy part of it remains lively and distinct in my grateful recollection. It was long before he consented to take me, but once he had consented, he devoted himself to me heart and soul. My school lessons, though I continued to do well in them, were now of secondary importance, and my private instruction became the main business. I had been used to attend all the classes in school regularly, but now I seldom went to lessons in arithmetic, drawing, and writing, spending these hours at home instead, under the supervision of my wise tutor. It is an odd fact that I was positively unable to learn mathematics. At first, Kartashevsky tried hard to teach me—and I cannot say that I did not understand his uncommonly clear explanations, but I forgot instantly what I had understood, so that he did not believe I had ever understood him. Knowing that I was intimate with Alexander Knyazhevich, the best mathematician in the school, my tutor suggested that he should try his hand with me. When Knyazhevich taught me, I understood him much better than my tutor, and I remembered the points longer. But it was of no avail: after a few days, not a single proposition, not a single proof, remained in my head. In respect of mathematics, my excellent memory proved no better than a clean sheet of white paper, which refused to retain a single mathematical sign! Therefore my tutor took into account my natural powers and inclinations, and drew up a course of education for me in accordance with them; it was to be general, not abstruse, and mainly literary. He wrote out a long list of books for me at once. As far as I can remember, this included Lomonosov, Derzhavin, Dmitriev, Kapnist, and Khemnitser. Kheraskov and Sumarokov I possessed already, but my tutor never read these with me. Then there were French books on the list: the preachers, Massillon, Flechier, and Bourdaloue; *The Arabian Nights*, *Don Quixote*, *The Death of Abel* and *The Idylls* of Gessner, *The Vicar of Wakefield*, and two *Natural Histories*, one of them with pictures, but I do not know the authors' names. To me natural history was the most seductive of the sciences. There were other books as well, but I forget their names too.

But the first thing my tutor did with me was to work at foreign languages, especially French, in which I, like most of the boys, was very weak; and in three months I could read it fluently and understand any French book. Words and the grammar and conversations I learned in the ordinary course at school, but at home I learned nothing by heart: my tutor took a book and made me read and translate aloud. At first I was completely puzzled, and this method seemed to me absurd and wearisome, but my teacher stuck to it, and I was soon surprised and delighted by its success. I made a separate list of words I did not know; then I wrote out a literal translation of the French, a rough copy and then a fair copy. I had the active memory of youth, and I was always able to repeat next morning, without having learned them, the French original, my Russian translation, and the separate list of words. The first piece I read and translated was *Les Aventures d'Aristonoy* from a French reading-book; next I began to read and translate *The Arabian Nights*, which was followed by *Don Quixote*. Certain passages I was forbidden to read, and I obeyed orders scrupulously. What a pleasure it was to have such delightful and attractive lesson-books! Even now, fifty years later, I recall these readings with the liveliest satisfaction; I remember how impatiently I awaited the time fixed for them, although it was nearly always immediately after dinner!

My tutor was a serious student of his own branch of science. Making use of the labors of men who were famous then in that branch of learning, he was writing an original course of lectures on Pure Mathematics to be delivered in the school. He knew modern languages very well and could write them readily; he read much German literature and philosophy. He was also constantly engaged in perfecting his knowledge of Latin, and his command of it astonished the University of Vilna with which he was connected later. To read *The Arabian Nights* and *Don Quixote* with me was a relief from his severer studies; and he joined heartily in my laughter, like a boy of my own age, or even like a child, and at first this puzzled me exceedingly. At such times my tutor was a different man: all his dryness and strictness disappeared, and I came to love him like an elder brother, though at the same time I stood in great awe of him.

When I had got a fair mastery of French, the reading of Russian authors, especially the poets, became our main occupation. My tutor explained poetry so well, pointing out the writer's meaning and the merits of his style, that my liking for literature soon became a passion. With no effort on my part, I learned by heart all the best poetry of Derzhavin, Lomonosov, and Kapnist, selected by the critical judgment of my teacher; and Dmitriev's poetry, which was then considered a model of style for purity and correctness, I could repeat almost from end to end. Of Russian prose we read very little, probably because my teacher was dissatisfied with the prose writers of the time. It is worthy of

remark that he read no Karamzin with me except a few letters from *The Russian Traveler*, and would not allow me to
have *My Trifles* among my books. But I knew already all
that Karamzin had written, and used to recite enthusiastically *The Parting of Hector and Andromache*, and *The Proof
of Solomon's Wisdom*. I proceeded at once to display these
acquirements to my tutor, but he only frowned and said that
the first poem gave no idea of Homer, and the second none
of Ecclesiastes; "Karamzin is no poet; better forget these
poems altogether," he added. I was exceedingly puzzled: I
admired both poems, and continued to recite them when I
happened to be by myself in the garden.

He did not allow me to compose, and I could only taste
this pleasure in secret or in Ibrahimov's class. My room was
divided by a thin partition from the drawing room, which
served my tutor as study and bedroom, and I once overheard a conversation about myself between him and Ibrahimov. The latter praised me highly and showed my tutor a
composition I had written in class, in the form of a letter to
a friend, on "The Beauties of Spring"; he added that it might
be as well to make me do more in the way of original composition. My tutor always exercised a kind of ascendancy
over his colleagues, and he now replied very positively, "My
dear fellow, that is all utter nonsense. The boy's essay is a
mere cento of phrases picked up out of different books; and
it is impossible to judge whether he has any original gift.
He has a great fancy for writing, and I am sure he will soon
begin to stain paper, but I shall keep him in leading-strings
as long as I can. The later he begins to write, the better for
my young Telemachus." (This was a nickname given to me
by all the masters, while they called my tutor "Mentor" or
"Minerva.") "A young man ought to collect good examples,
and form his taste by reading authors with a correct and

well-formed style. Do you suppose I let him read all Derzhavin? Not a bit of it! He only knows twenty poems of his, but he knows the whole of Dmitriev. I believe you will spoil him. I daresay you constantly use in school *Poor Lisa*, and *Natalya, the Nobleman's Daughter** and *Sofya, A Dramatic Fragment*." Ibrahimov was offended, and replied that, for all their charm, he understood perfectly that these works were unsuitable for boys. "Glad to hear it!" my tutor continued, "but these are the very poems which Erich has made them translate into French." (Erich, who had a great knowledge of languages, ancient and modern, used to teach French and German to the Senior Class.) This conversation went on for some time, and my youth did not prevent me from understanding the good sense of my tutor's arguments. He would not have talked so loudly about me if he had known that I was in the house. A teacher having failed to appear, I had come back early from school and passed unnoticed into my room. On this occasion I learned the high estimate Kartashevsky had formed of my mother; but alas! about myself he did not make a single flattering remark; yet how I longed to hear something of the kind! It really seemed as if he knew that I was listening behind the door.

When I reflect now upon the past, it puzzles me exceedingly, and I cannot understand why I was so warmly attached to my tutor. I was too young to appreciate fully the deep sympathy and real affection for me that were concealed under that dry manner. Never once did he show kind feeling, or flatter my vanity by any kind of compliment, or praise my diligence, and yet I loved him more than anyone outside my family. I remember that I once heard him laughing and looked into his room. He had some mathematical

* Novels by Karamzin.

treatise in his hand, and the stern martinet was laughing like a child as he watched some kittens at play; he wore an expression so kind and even affectionate that I was jealous of those kittens. When I went into the room with my book, his face changed and assumed the old expression—cold and composed, with even a trace of surliness.

And so my life went on. At times, my tutor became more approachable, and his manner of addressing me, if not friendly, was at least playful. This happened only when we were alone, and especially during the reading of *Don Quixote* —Sancho Panza was an inexhaustible source of laughter to us both—but the appearance of any third person, even if it was only Yevseich, at once put an end to his mirth.

Grigori Kartashevsky was the son of a Little Russian priest who had the rank of nobility and owned about a hundred serfs, and the great-grandson of a Turk who left Turkey for reasons unknown to me, became a Christian, and then married and settled down in Little Russia. In youth he was neglected by his mother; his father, who loved him with a mother's tenderness, seeing that the child was unhappy at home, took him to Moscow when he was nine years old, and placed him as a Government scholar at a school connected with the University. The son was passionately attached to his father. He suffered much when left alone at Moscow, and his joy and excitement, when his father visited him a year later, were so great that he fell ill of a fever, and the poor father, called back by his duties, had to leave his darling on a sickbed. A year later the father died. During the eighteen years that followed his entrance at the Moscow school, the boy paid only one visit to his home in Little Russia. This was shortly before he entered the teaching profession, and the impression left upon him by his visit was painful and distressing. All these facts I learned from his servant Yashka, who had come from Little Russia with his master. In my tutor's pronunciation, in his turn of mind, and in his appearance, there was no indication whatever of his native country, and I think it had no attraction for him. I often heard him praise the good sense of Great Russians and laugh at the indolence and stupidity of his own countrymen. This gave great offence to the other Little Russians, Zapolsky and Markevich. The latter was the school bursar, a fat and very good-natured man, a born humorist and very amusing; he was very kind to me, and I was very fond of him.

The spring of 1804 came round, and my tutor and I fasted in Passion Week and carried out all the observances prescribed by the Church for that season. Our parish church, dedicated to St. Barbara the Martyr, was close to the outside of Kazan, and the roads were in a terrible condition, owing to the thaw; yet we went on foot to all the services, even in the early morning. Zapolsky came to our house one day, and I happened to overhear him laughing at Kartashevsky for his devoutness. His words implied that my tutor had not always been equally strict in his performance of religious duties, but he got a sharp rebuke on this occasion for ill-timed jesting. Zapolsky, who set up for a freethinker, was much offended and did not come near us for a long time. I ought to say that Kartashevsky, during his whole life, was a sincere Christian. This tiff did not prevent my tutor from going with me to Zapolsky's country house, where we spent the time together very pleasantly, in the absence of the owners. We lived in a little wing of the house, on the bank of a large pond that had just lost its winter covering of ice; we read continually and took two walks every day, defying the mud. Spring distracted my attention and reminded me too much of spring at Aksakovo; the budding sportsman could not hear with indifference the cries of the returning birds. One day my tutor was reading some serious French book with me; he was sitting by the open window, trying to explain some idea that I could not quite grasp, when suddenly the musical cry of a redshank rang out, and the bird itself, with its wings raised and its slender red legs stretched out, alighted gracefully on the bank of the pond, right opposite the window. I started, dropped the book, and rushed to the window, to the astonishment of my tutor. "A redshank! A redshank!" I repeated breathlessly. "He perched on the bank close by! Look, there he is, walking about!" But Kartashevsky did not understand the feelings of a sportsman; he told me sharply to sit down and go on with my book. I obeyed, but, though I could not see the bird, I could hear its note; the blood rushed to my face, and I could not take in a word of what I was reading. My tutor was displeased. He told me to put the book down and write a fair copy of an old translation that he had already corrected; he took a book himself. An hour later he said, "Well, has the redshank flown out of your head by this time?" I said it had, and we resumed the work that had been interrupted. I should add that he was always indulgent on these occasions: whenever he saw that I was tired or inattentive, he made me do some mechanical task or sent me to walk in the garden.

Examinations began with the beginning of June. Though I did very well in all the classes I attended, yet, as I had dropped some subjects altogether, I got no prize; but this did not interfere with my promotion to the Senior Class. Only nine boys completed the course and left the school at this time; the rest remained, to spend another year in the same form.

A carriage and three horses arrived to fetch me. Yevseich and I got ready for the journey, and it was settled that we should start after dinner on Speech Day, which was on one of the early days of July. My tutor told me the day before that he would like to go part of the way with me, and asked whether I approved of this plan. I supposed that he would go as far as the town gate, and said that I should be very glad. Next morning Yevseich whispered in my ear, "He intends to go with us to Aksakovo, but he told me not to tell you." Though I worked willingly at school, I was not altogether pleased by this news. I was looking forward to a real orgy of fishing in the holidays, and even more to shooting, for my father had promised a year ago to get me a gun and teach me to shoot. But I knew that my tutor would not drop his lessons with me and would make heavy demands on my time, and also I was vexed with him for not telling me. Yevseich too seemed discontented. When Speech Day was over, we dined rather earlier than usual and drove out of the town. I pretended to be ignorant of my tutor's plan. When we had reached the country, we got out and walked for a time. My tutor was in very good humor and even gay; he looked with pleasure at the green fields and woods and the cloudlets in the summer sky. Suddenly he smiled and said, "This fine weather tempts me to go with you to your halt for the night; then I shall see you catch fish for our supper." Keeping up the pretence of ignorance, I said, "Very well! Then let us get in again and go faster, or we shall arrive late. But when will you turn back, and how do you mean to travel?" "Oh, I shall spend the night in the carriage with you, and hire a cart tomorrow morning," he replied, looking at me attentively. We got into the carriage and went off at a quick trot. The beauty of the evening was enchanting. We had fishing tackle with us, and Yevseich and I caught a quantity of fish, which was boiled or fried for our supper; then we lay down in the carriage to sleep.

Waking early next morning, I saw that we were moving; the sun was already high in the sky; my tutor was sitting in the carriage opposite to me, and I saw he was laughing. I burst out laughing myself and confessed that I had known his plan all the time. He scolded Yevseich for indiscretion; then, reading in my face that I was not quite pleased, he said, "You are afraid that I shall interfere with your amusements, but you need not fear that. I shall not give you lessons except when you ask me to do so yourself. We might just as well read something now, as there is nothing else to do in the carriage," and he pulled a book out of his pocket. I was quite comforted by his words and would gladly have embraced him, but I dared not even think of taking such a liberty. We did a great deal of work on that journey; besides, I repeated over again all that I had learned, and I talked much more, and more openly, than at Kazan; yet, wherever it was possible to fish, fish I did to my heart's content. So we traveled on till we reached Aksakovo on the fifth day. My tutor's visit was a most pleasant surprise to my mother; she was delighted to see him.

Though we did not at all expect it, we found the house full of relations and visitors and a great bustle going on. My aunt Tatyana was going to be married, and the wedding was fixed for a few days later. Though now past forty, she was very active and well preserved. She was tired of living in her brother's house in complete dependence upon her sister-in-law, who in days gone by had suffered much at the hands of her husband's sisters; and Tatyana, though she was better than the rest, was not guiltless. She wished to spend her old age at least under her own roof and to be mistress in her own house, however small that house might be. Her future husband was Vasili Uglichinin, who, after a life spent in the army, had recently retired as lieutenant colonel. He was a very simple and kindly man, of an honest and friendly nature. He was well over fifty, with nothing to live on but his pension; he belonged to a very poor but noble family, which had migrated to the district of Ufa. He had entered the army at fourteen and done good service in his quiet way—taking part in many engagements and receiving several slight wounds. He had struggled with poverty all his life and had earned no distinctions, though his formal discharge was so long and eloquent that his breast might well have been covered with medals. His last service had been in the Caucasus, and from there he had brought home a small sum saved out of his pay, a uniform without epaulets, a hill-pony so old that its coat had turned white, rheumatism in every joint, and a cataract in his right eye. The cataract was fortunately not very noticeable, and the old soldier took pains to hide it, fearing that the loss of an eye might make the bride draw back. My aunt had a small estate of twenty-five serfs, within seven versts of where her sister Alexandra lived, and a small house on the estate. The house, which was no more than two peasants' houses run together, stood on the bank of a stream that swarmed with trout—a great attraction in my eyes! She owned a suitable amount of excellent land with all the usual accessories— land that had been bought for her from the Bashkirs for almost nothing. To the retired soldier this modest domain seemed a haven of rest; and to an old man half a loaf was better than no bread.

There was much secret laughter at the expense of an old, one-eyed bridegroom, but my parents and my tutor took no share in it: they always treated him with respect and cordiality. Evil tongues accounted for my mother's behavior by saying that she wished to get rid of her sister-in-law. But that was false. My mother never failed in appreciation and respect for simple and guileless people; she honestly advised my aunt to marry this worthy man, and my aunt was grateful to her for that advice till the day of her death. Kartashevsky, who shared my mother's feeling, took special pleasure in conversing with the veteran, who was excessively silent as a rule, but readily answered his questions and told us much that was curious and entertaining. My tutor lost no time in enlisting my interest and sympathy for this character, explaining to me those merits that I was too young to notice and understand.

There was no room in the house for male visitors, and even the ladies were accommodated with difficulty, because three rooms were given up to the future bride and bridegroom. In this difficulty my mother took a step for which her husband's relations never forgave her. Her own bedroom, which no one outside the family ever dared even to enter, she gave up to my tutor and put me there with him; of course we left it as soon as the party broke up. The marriage took place with no hitch on the appointed day. My father went with the pair to their new abode but came back at once. At last we were left alone and had our house to ourselves.

But here I break the thread of my narrative to run on ahead a little. For the married life of my uncle and aunt rises up so vividly before me that I want to say something about it.

After her marriage, my aunt became familiar with the trouble of poverty, of which she had known nothing during her girlhood in her father's house or under the roof of my parents; but she was perfectly happy. She felt a tender and passionate love for her old colonel, and his love for her was no less deep and tender. Unfortunately they had no children. My aunt lived to be very old, but a kind of maidenly

modesty clung to her till the last. She was rather ceremoni-
ous in addressing her husband and suppressed every sign of
affection for him when a third person was present, though
the old soldier would sometimes give a sly hint that the lady
was not always quite so prudish. Be that as it may, in company they were always distant and polite to one another,
never saying "thou" but always "you." A casual observer
might have taken this for coldness, but soon one became
aware of a different state of things—a solicitous attention
on both sides, a constant observation, an instant sympathy
in each other's every word and movement—and it became
clear to all that husband and wife drew from each other the
very breath of life. If there was any difference in their feeling, it was that the husband's love was less easily alarmed.
Their little house shone like a new pin; it breathed of peace
and attracted the visitor by its coziness. It cannot be said
that they had similar tastes, but, in their case, differences
only met to make the course of life run more smoothly. For
example, my aunt liked cats and dogs in the house, and it
must be stated that her pets, for some reason, were guilty of
no nuisance and never tore or spoiled anything belonging to
her. My uncle did not like them at all; yet even Kalmyck, a
hideous lapdog that snuffled and lolled out its tongue at one
corner of its mouth, was pleasant and actually dear to him,
because she loved it, and he fed and caressed this repulsive
animal with satisfaction and gratitude. Then there was a
marmot that passed the winter under the stove; it was the
source of much amusement to my aunt and as much annoyance to my uncle, because it carried off his slippers and hid
them so cleverly that they were often missing for a whole
day, and the poor colonel had to step out of bed in the morning with bare feet; yet even the marmot enjoyed his favor. In

their little house everything was in its place, and everything seemed to be somehow better than in other people's houses: their dogs and cats were sleeker and cleaner, the cage-birds sang louder and more gaily, their plants were greener. If you gave them some half-withered stick in a flowerpot, the plant at once revived, put forth green leaves, and grew so splendidly that you wanted to have it back again. In her small rooms, my aunt grew vines from seed, palms, and other plants that need heat. The atmosphere seemed to have something calming and life-giving in it, something suited to beast and plant, which made up in some degree for the loss of freedom or native climate. Together they attended to the management of their small estate, and without any pressure on their part, all the work was done twice as quickly and twice as well as it was done elsewhere. Together they walked out to pick mushrooms and berries; together they angled for the fine trout in their little stream; and together they rejoiced over each fish they caught. But, if one of them chanced to have a slight illness, what was the state of matters then! At once there came to the surface that deep and tender mutual affection which might easily escape notice in the ordinary course of life.

But I shall refrain from further details that might carry me too far afield. I shall only say that, when later in life I sometimes paid a visit to this remote corner and watched for a few hours this simple modest existence, it always made a deep impression upon me, and I wondered whether this was not the true happiness for man—a life without passions and excitements, a life undisturbed by insoluble questions and unsatisfied desires. The peace and order of their life remained long with me; I felt a vague agitation and regret for the lack of something so near at hand and so easily procured; but, whenever I put to myself the question, "Would you like to be what your uncle is?"—I was afraid to reply, and my feeling of agitation vanished instantly.

My father kept his promise to me: he had got me a light gun, very handy in the stock and prettily finished. It was inlaid with silver, the sights were of silver, and the barrel tapered like those of the English guns then used by sportsmen. He had picked it up for fifteen rubles, but, though only of Tula manufacture,* it was worth two or three times as much, even at the prices of those days. It did very good work at fifty yards. With my first shot I killed a crow, and that settled my fate: I went mad over shooting. Next day I shot a duck and two snipe, and my madness was confirmed. Fishing and hawking were forgotten; carried away by my natural excitability, I ran about with the gun all that day and dreamed of the gun all night. It was just the same on the days that followed. My tutor never saw me except for a moment, and then I was busy and in a hurry; he looked forward to a time when I should ask him for some work to do, but that time never came.

He then told my mother of our agreement, and she issued her orders to me: I was to ask my tutor to set me some tasks to be done under his supervision for two hours every day. Though this requirement went much against the grain, I obeyed. At first my tutor could not help laughing at my dismal and dejected figure. I opened a French book and began to translate, but I was too distracted to attend to what I was reading: visions of ducks and snipe passed before my eyes, and their cries rang in my ears. When I began to blunder in translating, my tutor frowned, took the book from me, and walked about the room from corner to corner for

* Tula was once the manufacturing center of Russia.

a whole hour, giving me a serious lecture and urging me to conquer the dangerous habit that made me forget everything else in my passionate devotion to some amusement. But alas! I neither heard nor understood a single word; his eloquent phrases, just sentiments, and convincing arguments, were all wasted. Seeing that his appeal had failed, he tried another plan: he left me in perfect freedom for a whole week, to run about with my gun from morning till night, till I was tired out and fit to drop. He hoped that I should come round of myself, that bodily fatigue and an overdose of this new amusement would restore me to my senses. But he was mistaken. I ate little and slept badly; I grew as brown as a gypsy and lost flesh visibly; but I never stopped shooting.

But now my tutor, fearing for my health, took decisive steps, which my mother had suggested some time before, though she wished to leave my tutor a free hand: my gun was hung up on the wall, and I was forbidden to go out shooting. I am both amused and ashamed when I think of the way I spent the first twenty-four hours. I cried and even yelled like a child of three; I rolled on the floor and tore my hair; I very nearly tore up my books and papers; indeed nothing but my mother's grief and my father's gentle remonstrance saved me from acting like a fool and a madman. Next day I came to myself, as it were, and on the third day I was able to study and to read my favorite poets aloud with attention and enjoyment. On the fourth day I had calmed down altogether, and then the cloud lifted for the first time from the face of my tutor. Till then he had hardly spoken to me; he had only looked at me with an expression either of displeasure or of insulting pity. But now he showed sympathy for me and spoke words of indulgence and wisdom; and this time his efforts were entirely successful. Angry with myself and ashamed almost to tears, I now ran from one extreme to the other and wished to give up the gun for good. But this did not please him either: he disapproved of my intention and insisted that I should go out shooting every day from breakfast to dinner or from dinner till evening, but that I should work diligently three or four hours a day, especially at history and geography, in which I was rather weaker than my chief rivals at school. And so the time flowed by in pleasant and regular occupation.

During this month it was possible for my parents to enjoy frank and friendly conversation with Kartashevsky without interruptions; and this increased their appreciation and regard for him, in whom penetrating intellect and high qualities of character were combined with many-sided culture and sound learning. My mother used all her power over me to make me understand the character of the man whom fortune had appointed to be my instructor. She considered this to be a special instance of God's goodness. I understood her meaning, and I had a strong feeling of the truth of her words. I assured her—though unfortunately I could never quite convince her—that I was myself warmly attached to him; that, though my attention was distracted at home by my favorite pursuits and especially by the hitherto unknown delights of shooting, at Kazan my one thought was to gain the love and approval of my tutor, and one kind word from him made me entirely happy.

My dear sister, who was also my bosom friend, was growing taller and prettier at a surprising rate. Though she could no longer share my outdoor amusements and occupations or spend so much of her time with me, she bore this deprivation patiently when she saw how happy I was; but she complained of the time I spent over lessons, and this was probably the reason why she did not look with favor on my teacher.*

We left Aksakovo on the 10th of August and arrived at Kazan on the 15th without any misadventures. It was a surprise to me when Kartashevsky that same day told me not to attend classes in the school, and made out a program of work for me to do at home. But he went off himself every morning to meetings of the Governors and stayed there a long time; he acted as their honorary secretary. Five days later, he told me that many of the boys had not turned up yet and there was little doing in the way of teaching; then he proposed that we should go to Zapolsky's country house, to enjoy an extra holiday and do some work for a week or so. This was a still greater surprise, but I was much pleased. In the country, we spent not a week, but more than a fortnight; my tutor drove to Kazan several times, starting early and returning for a late dinner. I asked no questions about these visits. We returned at last to Kazan, and he told me the next day to begin my attendance at school. I went off in good spirits, but my schoolfellows met me with glum faces and told me of an unfortunate affair that had taken place. I shall tell it here.

I should begin by saying that Likhachov, the Rector of the school, was a very bad Rector and also the possessor of a ludicrous personality, which was not calculated to inspire respect: for one thing, his lower lip was as large and swollen as if it had been bitten by a poisonous fly or stung by a wasp. Neither masters nor boys had any respect for him; and even before I went home for the summer holidays, he was hooted by the boys one day when he was walking about the dining

---

* Yet she became his wife twelve years later. (See footnote on page 91.)

hall during dinner; the cause of irritation was the quality of the porridge, in which some boy had found a piece of tallow candle. That same night, inscriptions abusing the Rector, boldly written with red pencil in large printed characters, appeared on many of the inside walls, on the outer walls, and even on the cupola of the building. These inscriptions were so high up that the artist must have used a ladder, and the inscription on the cupola was recognized as a triumph of boldness and agility. Neither then nor later were the culprits discovered; even now I do not know who did the writing. And now for later events.

A few days before I returned with my tutor from Aksakovo, and when most of the boys had already come back, an official, known for some reason as "quartermaster," who had once served in the army and controlled all the old soldiers employed about the school, got angry with one of his subordinates and proceeded to thrash him without mercy. This took place in the back yard, which was divided from the front yard, where the boys could play in their free time, by a wooden boarding; and as it was after dinner, the boys were all there at the time. The sufferer's loud cries aroused such pity in their young hearts that Alexander Knyazhevich and some other boys of the Senior Class passed through the gate into the back yard, in contravention of the rules, and called loudly on the quartermaster to drop his stick. But this attack on his authority made the man furious. He began to shout abuse in the foulest terms at the boys; Alexander Knyazhevich, a very kind-hearted boy and therefore more excited than the rest, as he was in front, bore the brunt of all this bad language. When the noise of the contention reached their ears, all the Senior Class made an appearance in the back yard, and others followed them. The elder Knyazhevich, Dmitri, recognizing the voice of his brother to whom he was much attached, was the first to hurry to the scene; naturally hot-tempered, he eagerly espoused the cause of his insulted brother, and the other boys backed him with one accord. As may be supposed, there was no lack of forcible expressions and threats; the quartermaster soon found himself obliged to drop his disciplinary proceedings and beat a hasty retreat. This trifling incident, due to a praiseworthy feeling of pity for suffering and then to reasonable anger at grossly insolent language, led to very lamentable consequences, simply because it was misunderstood and mismanaged by the Rector.

The Senior Class began by submitting a humble petition in writing: they asked that the quartermaster should be dismissed for cruelty and insolence. The Rector refused to grant this petition. He threw all the blame on the boys and even sentenced some of them to some form of punishment. This injustice naturally produced irritation: their respectful petition had been refused, and now the boys took to persistent demands and infringements of the established rules. The Senior Class struck work and refused to attend any classes until their enemy was removed from the school; and the other two forms soon made common cause with their seniors. As the trouble was chiefly due in its origin to the insulting language addressed to Alexander Knyazhevich, it was natural that his brother, Dmitri, who took the lead in every department of school life and was very popular, should become the leader of this movement. The Rector played a cowardly part: he dared not show himself to the boys; and when he had to attend a meeting of the Governors, he came by a back entrance, passing through Yakovkin's rooms; but he sent various envoys to remonstrate with the rebels, and all these remonstrances proved ineffectual. Upadishevsky was loved for his kindness and respected by the boys; and if he had been acting as Head Master at the time, the whole of this unfortunate affair would have been smothered at birth; but he had gone away some weeks earlier owing to ill health, and his substitute was a mere cipher.

For three days the affair dragged on in the same unsettled state. On the fourth day, the boys found out that the Rector was attending a meeting of the Governors; they first posted a guard at the back entrance and then proceeded in a body to the door of the board room, where they loudly demanded that the quartermaster should be discharged. The Rector tried to leave the building, but was told that his line of retreat was cut off by the boys posted at the back door. This news threw him into such alarm and agitation that he gave orders on the spot to draw up a resolution for the discharge of the offending quartermaster; and the resolution was read out to the boys. The effect was immediate: the rebels calmed down at once, expressed their thanks to the authorities, and ceased from their mutinous behavior. Order was restored, and the ordinary routine of school life began again. At first it was supposed that this incident would not lead to any further developments; but this belief was quite mistaken. The Rector reported the case at once in the highest quarters, and then, acting on some advice, he entered into relations with the Governor of Kazan, and took the following measures. A few days later, during dinnertime, a party of soldiers armed with rifles and bayonets entered the hall, and were followed immediately by the Governor and the Rector. The latter then called out by name sixteen boys of the Senior Class, including of course the elder Knyazhevich, and ordered them to be taken to the school prison under the escort of armed soldiers. All the other boys were horror-struck, and dead silence reigned in the hall. Two soldiers armed with bayonets were posted at each outer door of the school, and four at the door of the prison.

I heard the whole story a fortnight after it occurred, when I came back after the holidays, or, I should say, when I returned from Zapolsky's house and joined the depleted ranks of the Senior Class to which I now belonged. The other boys told me the bad news at once. And now it flashed upon me why my prudent tutor had first prevented me from going into school and then carried me off with him to the country. Had I been on the spot, I should beyond all doubt have been one of the most active sharers in this unlucky affair. Six weeks later the decision of the central authority was delivered at Kazan. Again the Governor appeared in the dining hall, accompanied by the Rector and other Governors of the school; a document was read, setting forth the guilt of the rebellious boys and declaring that, as an example to the rest, eight of the Senior Class, who were considered the ringleaders, were expelled from the school without a certificate of character. The victims were the best students of the class; Dmitri Knyazhevich, who was one of the eight, we considered the ornament and pride of the school. We were all deeply impressed and sorely grieved by the sentence; when it had been executed, the sentries were withdrawn, and the state of siege, which we strongly resented, came to an end.

The Rector was removed from his place soon afterwards, and was succeeded by the senior teacher, Yakovkin. Dmitri Knyazhevich long kept up a close connection with his schoolfellows. He entered the public service at Petersburg, and wrote to his brother by every post; sometimes he addressed his communications to us all, and then his letters were solemnly read aloud in the hearing of the whole form. After a period of sadness and silence, the youthful population of the school began by degrees to recover their spirits and to forget the painful affair: the old noisy activity returned, the old laughing and singing was heard again, and life sped forward as if nothing had happened.

My work in school and at home went on quietly till midwinter under the steady supervision and direction of my tutor; but at that time my uncle Alexander, my mother's brother, paid a visit to Kazan and took me twice to the theater, of course with my tutor's permission. We saw an opera and a comedy—the latter was called *A Sister Sold by a Brother*—and the effect of these two performances upon me was nearly as strong as the effect of my first day's shooting. I had a special passion for dramatic compositions, and had formed from what I had heard some notion of their performance upon the stage. But the reality far surpassed my anticipation. The two performances I had seen filled my head day and night, and I found it utterly impossible to concentrate my attention upon my books. Of course my tutor noticed this at once, and his questions soon elicited the true reason. He frowned and showed displeasure at this new folly on my part, and once more I had to listen to a long lecture. But I felt the justice of his rebukes this time; for I understood the danger of my inclination to be carried away beyond all bounds by the things I cared for. My passion for the theater was the natural development of a tendency that had shown itself from early years in my love of recitation and of plays, both Russian and French; but I made a great effort and succeeded in checking the rising flame. I calmed down and applied myself with more than ordinary zeal to my tasks.

My tutor was much pleased. When a week had passed, he started a conversation about the stage and the art of acting in which he gave me some real notion of the subject and told me stories of many famous actors, both living and dead, Russians and foreigners; for instance, I heard of the Moscow actors, Shusherin and Plavilshchikov. These conversations, so delightful to me, went on for three days during the hours of recreation. Then, one happy day, when I had come back from school and was drinking my evening tea, my tutor opened my door and said in a cheerful voice, "You have got to drive somewhere with me at once. Be quick and get done with that milk and water!" (I was very fond of milk and used to put so much in my tea that my tutor often called it milk and water.) I was ready in a moment, and we got into a sledge and started. I felt sure that we were going to call on M. Voskresensky; his son was at school with me, and my tutor sometimes took me to their house. At a turning, the driver was told to go straight down Georgia Street; I was surprised, for this was not the way I expected. A few minutes later we were opposite the theater, and the order came, "To the theater entrance." When we got there, my tutor sprang out of the sledge, but I was so stunned by the joyful prospect that I sat stock-still. He could not help laughing, "Well," he said, "don't you want to come?" and I took a flying leap to the ground. Tickets had been taken beforehand; we went in and sat together in the front row of the stalls. An opera called *The Pork Butchers* was performed. How intensely I enjoyed that evening! At this moment I can see before me Mikhail Kalmikov who played the leading part of the old pork-butcher; and I can hear Pritkov singing to the guitar, though in fact he only opened his mouth while an actress behind the scenes sang the music, and I remember some of the words:

O loved one in whose chains I lie,
Hark to thy pris'ner's plaintive cry!

Yet more than fifty years have passed since that evening, and during all that time I have never once heard the opera of *The Pork Butchers* mentioned!

On our way home I thanked my tutor heartily, and he pleased me by saying that this treat was a reward for my sensible behavior, and that, if *The Pork Butchers* did not upset me, he would take me to the theater from time to time. To tell the truth, *The Pork Butchers* did fill my thoughts and upset me to some extent, but I tried hard to hide my state of mind, and got on so well with my work, thanks to an exceptionally strong memory, that my tutor remained quite in the dark. In the course of a short time I saw a good many plays— *The Hobbledehoy, Mistakes, or Morning Thoughts are Wisest*, an opera called *Nina, or The Crazed Lover*, and *Count Valtron*, a play by Kotzebue. My love of the stage grew and strengthened every day. I learned by heart the plays I had seen, and found time to perform all the parts with myself for audience. Of this my tutor knew nothing, for I shut myself up in my own room for the purpose, or used a part of the house which was uninhabited and unheated.

In this winter of 1804 I began a friendship with another pensioner at the school, Alexander Panayev, who was, like me, a lover of the stage and of Russian literature. Being a worshipper of Karamzin, he wrote prose idylls, in which he tried to reproduce the smooth and florid style created by the historian. His brother Ivan was a lyric poet. Alexander Panayev was editor at that time of a manuscript magazine called *Shepherds of Arcadia*, of which I still preserve several issues. All the contributors signed their writings with pastoral names—Adonis, Daphnis, Amyntas, Iris, Damon, Palaemon, and so on. As Alexander Panayev was a skillful penman and artist, he used to write and illustrate with his own hand each monthly issue of his magazine. To tell the truth, as we were children then, so was our national literature in its childhood; but it is worth remarking that the tendency and style of this magazine were exactly the same as those which prevailed in Russia for some decades after this date.

I took no share in the editing of the magazine, because, thanks to the exertions of my tutor, I was not yet an author. But alas! the example proved very seductive, and I began to write a little in secret, though I kept it even from my bosom friend, Panayev. A year later, he and I were joint editors of another magazine, which will be described hereafter. In this same winter amateur theatricals took place in the school; a tiresome priggish play whose name I forget was performed twice, and also a little comedy by Sumarokov, *A Dowry Gained by Deceit.* I was only a spectator, for many older boys wished to act, and also I did not venture even to hint at such a step to my tutor. But the next year, which was to bring about a development of my dramatic and literary doings at school, proved that I was mistaken about my tutor's feelings.

For nearly a year, reports had been going about that a University was to be founded at Kazan. The reports turned out to be true, and in December 1804 the official announcement was received that a charter for the University had been signed by the Emperor on the 5th of November. A Chancellor was appointed, Stepan Rumovsky, a high political official, and he came to Kazan. This event, which caused much excitement in the town, was even more interesting to the school and especially to the Senior Class. Meetings were held daily, with Rumovsky as chairman; the other members were Professor Herman and Professor Zeppelin who had come with the Chancellor, Yakovkin, the Rector of the school, and all the senior teachers. Of their proceedings I and my schoolfellows knew nothing. But one evening there was a large dinner party at my tutor's house, which included the two outside professors, the Chancellor's secretary, and all the senior teachers of the school except Yakovkin. They met at a fairly late hour, when I was already in bed. It was a gay and noisy party and kept me awake for a long time, as I listened to them talking loudly and exchanging congratulations: they were speaking of the new University and of the appointment of teachers in the school to be professors and assistant professors. Next morning Yevseich told me that the party went on till three in the morning, that a great deal of wine and punch had been drunk, and that many of the guests were decidedly cheerful when they left. He added that Kartashevsky, though he had been forced to drink a great deal, showed no sign of it—"was not drunk even in one eye" was the precise expression of Yevseich. Never had our sober mansion witnessed such a scene before, and Yevseich and I were very much surprised, but the cause of it was now clear. Yevseich had overheard—and indeed I could tell him as much myself—that my tutor was appointed assistant professor in the new University, together with Zapolsky, Levitsky, and Erich. From their conversation I learned further that Yakovkin had been appointed to a full professorship of Russian History, and was also to act as inspector of Government students. His colleagues unanimously disapproved of this appointment: they thought Yakovkin deficient in learning and that he had not earned such rapid promotion. They were talking about the students, when I heard my tutor say in a loud voice, "For my Telemachus, gentlemen, I will go bail." I guessed at once that it was intended to admit me to the University. Such a thing was quite beyond my hopes, because I had not completed the course in the Senior Class and also knew no mathematics.

My tutor was still in bed when I went to school next morning. I made haste to tell the news to my companions, but they had all heard it already from Yakovkin's son, a very stupid and terribly fat boy. He boasted that he would be admitted too, but we all laughed at the idea. The top boys in the Senior Class, who had gone through the course of study twice, naturally hoped for promotion to student rank, but no one dreamed that I and some others would be chosen. But the list of students was published that same day, and it appeared that all the boys of the Senior Class, with two or three exceptions, were to enter the University; Yakovkin and I were both included. Strictly speaking, about a dozen of us, of whom I was certainly one, did not deserve to be admitted, partly because we were too young, and partly because we did not know enough. Nor do I refer merely to the fact that none of us knew Latin and very few, German, though in the coming autumn we were bound to attend lectures delivered in both languages. For all this, we rejoiced heartily and gave loud expression to our feelings. We embraced and congratulated one another and vowed to work untiringly at the subjects in which we were deficient, so that we should not be ashamed in the course of a few months to call ourselves qualified students of a University. A Latin class was started at once, and most of the future students began to tackle the language. From some foolish prejudice against Latin, I did not follow this praiseworthy example. To this day I do not understand why my tutor, who was a good Latin scholar himself, allowed me to shirk that subject.

I have a sense of satisfaction and of admiration when I recall the spirit which then animated the older boys, a spirit of genuine devotion to knowledge. They worked by night as well as by day till the effect was visible in their thin and altered faces. It was necessary for the authorities to take active measures, in order to discourage such excessive zeal: a master patrolled the dormitories all night to put out candles and forbid conversation, for even in the dark the boys examined each other in the subjects they had gone through. The teachers too were spurred on by the eager zeal of their pupils and worked with them, not in school only but in all free hours and on all holidays. My tutor gave a course of lectures on Applied Mathematics at his house for the best mathematicians, and this example was followed by his colleagues. Even after the college was opened, this state of things continued during the first year. Those were proud and happy days, days of pure love for knowledge and praiseworthy enthusiasm! I can speak of them impartially, for I did not share the eager aspirations that filled most of the scholars and exhibitioners. For some reason the pensioners stood somewhat aloof from the movement, and my own education went on as usual under the direction of my tutor. I dare say he thought I had no vocation for a learned life, and I dare say he was mistaken. He was led to this conclusion by my passion for literature and the drama, which had now come to the surface. But I believe that I could have conceived an equally strong passion for Natural History, and I might perhaps have done something useful in that line. My parents, however, never intended me for a scholar's life, against which they actually had a prejudice; and my tutor was only carrying out their wishes in the direction he gave to my studies.

It must be admitted that the birth of our University was somewhat premature. Six weeks after the Chancellor's arrival, on the 14th of February 1805, it was formally opened. The staff comprised only six teachers, of whom two were professors, Yakovkin and Zeppelin, while the other four, Kartashevsky, Zapolsky, Levitsky, and Erich, had the rank of assistants.

In that year, 1805, the letters from Dmitri Knyazhevich, which were always received by us and listened to with keen interest, became more interesting than ever, for political reasons. The first war with Napoleon was then going on, and news of the campaign was for some reason very scanty and very slow in reaching us, but Knyazhevich sent us early and full details. Besides this, his letters were so full of patriotic ardor and devotion to the glory of the Russian arms that they had an electric effect on all of us. When Alexander Knyazhevich called out, "A letter from my brother!" we needed no further summons—an eager crowd gathered round him at once, and leaning on each other's shoulders, in dead silence broken at times by enthusiastic shouts, we listened greedily while the letter was read aloud. Even the boys from the school joined us and listened to these letters. The famous General Bagration was our hero; and when we heard how he and his detachment, when left at the mercy of the enemy, had forced their way through the whole French army,* the cheers which we raised, and the passionate enthusiasm of every one of us, are beyond my powers of description. There was plenty of life in the young men of that day, and it is comforting to think of it now.

---

* After the battle of Hollabrunn (November 1805). Bagration fell at the battle of Borodino (1812).

The usual summer examinations were not held either in the school or the University, and all our time was spent in preparing for the courses of lectures to be delivered after our return. My tutor, for some reason unknown to me, sent me off for my holidays shortly before Speech Day. I traveled with Yevseich to Old Aksakovo in the Province of Simbirsk, where my family was then living. The reason for this migration was also unknown to me, but I did not like it at all. Old Aksakovo was ill-supplied with water; there was no fishing there and very little shooting. There was indeed plenty of black game, and it was possible to pick up a woodcock; but this difficult form of sport was still beyond my powers. Being aware of this beforehand, I laid in a stock of plays, intending to read them at leisure, and even to act them with my family for audience; I carried out this intention later with great pleasure and success. My parents, though they found it hard to believe, were much pleased that I was to enjoy the dignity of a student, and expressed regret that my tutor had not kept me till Speech Day, to hear the list of students formally read, and to receive my sword with the others. My dear sister was delighted to have me back at home. She listened with pleasure when I recited or rather acted my plays; tragedy, comedy, and even opera—all came alike to me, and I played all the parts, both male and female, changing my voice to a lisp or a squeak, singing bass or falsetto, and sometimes dressing up in clothes that I fished up out of old wardrobes. I had another occupation as well. As I knew that after the middle of August I should attend lectures on Natural History delivered by Professor Fuchs who had lately come to Kazan, I determined to collect butterflies and made a start in that direction during the holidays. My sister helped me in this, but alas! I destroyed a great num-

ber of these lovely creatures, because I did not know then
how to set and dry butterflies.

Twice during the holidays we traveled to Chufarovo and
spent a week each time in the house of my great-aunt, Praskovya Ivanovna Kurolyesova. The distance from Old Aksakovo was not more than forty or fifty versts. Praskovya
Ivanovna was much pleased to hear that I had become a
student: she announced the fact with pride to every visitor.
She made me put on my uniform, and was very sorry that I
had not got my sword, and she went so far as to give me ten
rubles to buy books. Of my dramatic activity no one would
have dared to tell her directly, for it was possible that she
might not have approved of it, but she happened to hear it
mentioned and made me recite, act, and sing. To my great
joy, she was much pleased and laughed a great deal. She
had never been in a theater in her life, but she was quick
at picking up things, and this new form of entertainment
suited her gay and lively temperament. But she liked my
ordinary reading better still. Sometimes when she was at
a loss for occupation, especially in winter—when she was
tired of playing cards and singing the songs and ballads of
those days, and tired of listening to gossip and scandal—she
made someone read aloud recent novels and tales; but she
never found a reader to suit her: even my mother, who was
better than others, did not give entire satisfaction. But when
she heard me, she said, "Well, that is something like reading!"—and from that day, though it was summer and she
generally spent the season in her splendid garden, she made
me read to her for at least two hours every day. *The Miller*
by Ablesimov, and *The Hawker* by Knyazhnin were sometimes chosen, and I remember her hearty good-humored
laughter, when she saw a mere boy representing one of the

two old men from whom these comedies take their titles. I gained a full measure of her good graces, and this was a great satisfaction to my family; for thoughts of the great fortune that she had promised to leave us could not be entirely banished from the anticipations and calculations which no man can help making. When I left, I received a gracious command from Praskovya Ivanovna to write to her twice a month, and she got those letters regularly down to the time of her death.

4

~

Life at College

I returned with no mishaps to Kazan and was much pleased to see my tutor again, and he greeted me affectionately. My first business was to get the sword that was part of my uniform and had been kept in store for my arrival. Alexander Panayev and I fastened on our swords and spent the whole of that Sunday walking about the streets of the town. As our costume was then a novelty, we had the satisfaction of attracting the attention and interest of the inhabitants, though some menservants, as they sat at the doors and courted the maids, being more sophisticated than the rest of their class, made bad jokes at our expense. The officers of the school had much business on their hands: students and boys were both lodged in the same building, and separate dormitories had to be arranged for the students, as well as separate meals in a second, smaller dining hall, and a scheme of University lectures had to be organized. By the end of August all arrangements were made, and lectures began as follows: Kartashevsky lectured on advanced Pure Mathematics, Zapolsky on Applied Mathematics and Experimental Physics, Levitsky on Logic and Philosophy,

Yakovkin on Russian History, Geography, and Statistics, Professor Zeppelin on General History, Professor Fuchs on Natural History, Professor Herman on Latin Literature and Antiquities, Erich on Greek and Latin Literature, and Evest—an assistant professor from a foreign University—on Chemistry and Anatomy. There was another professor, Buhnemann, a stout man who lectured in French on "The Law of Nature and of Nations." I attended his lectures but I have not the faintest recollection of them. Such was the rudimentary staff with which our University opened; nor were the faculties properly distinct. Yakovkin, being both inspector of the students and Rector of the school, enjoyed the title and authority of Vice-Chancellor; as chairman of the school Governors, who included all the professors and assistant professors, he controlled the educational department of school and University alike. The business administration was managed by the school office; Yakovkin was head of this also, and one of the university instructors acted regularly as secretary. With the permission of the Chancellor required by the rules of subordination, Yakovkin allotted chambers to the students and made other necessary arrangements. Many students, of whom I was one, had not completed the school course and continued to attend advanced classes there as well as college lectures; I was very glad of this, because it would have pained me to part from Ibrahimov. He loved me so sincerely and took such pains with me that the time spent in his classroom remains as one of the pleasantest memories of my youth. I ought to confess that he gave me more than my share of his attention and that my vanity, excited and gratified by his notice of me before the whole class, played a considerable part in the matter. Thus the transition from school to college was felt by us all, and especially by those who, like myself, continued to attend some classes in the school.

After the University opened, my friendship with Alexander Panayev, now a student like myself, grew by leaps and bounds, and soon there was such an intimacy between us as can only exist in early manhood; he, however, was eighteen and consequently three years older than I. My tutor approved of this friendship. Our love of literature and the stage was one of the ties between us, and we soon acquired another taste in common, for natural history and the collection of butterflies, though it was not till the following spring that this taste was fully developed.

During that winter the theater attracted us to the exclusion of everything else, and this was due to the unexpected appearance of a famous actor from Moscow, Plavilshchikov. His visit had a great influence on me. My tutor had spoken to me about him before this time, and now he gave me leave beforehand to go to the theater every night that Plavilshchikov was playing. He was much pleased that I should see a real artist and hear that correct, natural, and powerful delivery for which Plavilshchikov was justly famous. To go often to the pit or stalls was beyond the means of the students: a seat in the pit cost a ruble, and a stall two and a half rubles. Our regular resort was the gallery, where the price of entrance was two kopecks.* But for us the gallery had one serious drawback: as the play began at 6:30 P.M. and our lectures ended at 6:00, there was only just time to run to the theater and get a place on the back benches of the gallery, from which it was impossible to see anything, because the front rows were filled long before the performance began.

* A kopeck was worth one-hundredth of a ruble.

But we devised measures to overcome this difficulty. Two or sometimes three students, the biggest and strongest of us, used to go to the theater at five or earlier; there they sat down at the ends of an empty bench and kept off all intruders. The rest of us turned up just before the curtain rose and took the seats reserved for us. At first there were some disputes caused by this maneuver, but the regular visitors to the gallery soon became accustomed to the arrangement, and everything went off peaceably. Our emissaries at first concealed their disappearance from the classroom, but many of the professors and teachers, when they came to understand the reason, used to wink at the departure of some of their listeners. The good-natured Ibrahimov would often say, "Well, gentlemen, isn't it time to be off to the theater?" and sometimes dismissed his class half an hour too early. To procure playbills was the duty of the pensioner students. In those days there were no printed playbills at Kazan; written bills were supplied from the box office to a few persons of distinction, while the public was informed of the title of the play and the names of the actors by a notice secured by four tacks to a pillar or the wall of the main entrance to the theater. I must confess that we used to steal these notices. The method was this: You went up to the theater steps and began to read the notice; then, as soon as the coast was clear, you tore it off, hid it in your pocket, and carried your prize back to college. When Yesipov, the manager, discovered this trick of the students, he gave permission for them to get a playbill regularly from the box office.

To me, Plavilshchikov's acting was the revelation of a new world in dramatic art. Unable, especially at first, to see his defects, I was equally enchanted by him in tragedy, comedy, and melodrama. But he stayed a long time in Kazan and produced many new pieces, including his comedy *The Outcast*, which was a great success, and his tragedy *Yermak*, which had no merit and failed entirely; and, as he sometimes repeated the same part two or three times, we had plenty of opportunity for judging his acting and came to see that he was far better in some parts than in others. But his real triumphs in delivery were the parts of Titus in *The Mercy of Titus* and of the pastor in *Lovers' Vows*.* The latter performance was a perfect marvel to me. The part used to be played at Kazan by a very bad actor, Maxim Gulyaev, and was thought so intolerably dull by me and all the audience that the long monologue addressed by the pastor to Baron Neuhof was cut down by general desire to a few lines. Plavilshchikov restored the part to its full importance and simply killed all the other parts. It was really a masterly performance. Another play which he staged at Kazan was *Oedipus at Athens*, and his acting as Oedipus was rapturously applauded.

In him I saw for the first time truth, simplicity, and nature upon the stage, and it was a revelation to me. I felt all the faults of my own manner of recitation and eagerly set about reforming my delivery. My tutor had said something of the kind to me and had suggested improvements, but I hardly understood him. Now, however, the moment I heard Plavilshchikov in his best parts, I understood what my tutor found amiss in my performance—which shows how much better example is than the very best precepts. Directed by my tutor, I worked hard at this difficult task for a fortnight and then recited to my friend Alexander Panayev the long monologue from the pastor's part. He was struck dumb with astonishment; all he could say was "You're as

---

* Readers of Jane Austen will remember that *Lovers' Vows* was the play rehearsed but never acted at Mansfield Park.

good as Plavilshchikov! You're better!" Getting to college before me that day, he told them all of his new discovery, and when I came in to attend lectures, the students crowded round me and made me recite the monologue and passages that I knew by heart from other plays. If they did not call me a Plavilshchikov, they applauded me warmly, and some of the senior students at once conceived the idea of getting up plays ourselves. The authorities would not agree to this all at once; therefore Panayev and I put together a play of a kind—it was childishly silly, of course—and acted it, with the aid of his brothers, in the rooms which they occupied; they lived in a biggish stone house belonging to their uncle. The title and plot of this play I have forgotten, but I remember that I played two parts in it—an old hermit in the first two acts and a robber-chief, who is killed by a pistol shot, in the third. I distinguished myself chiefly as the hermit.

Our Chancellor lived in Petersburg, and it was long before we received permission from him to make a theater with scenery and footlights in one of the University halls. In the meantime, we got permission from the Vice-Chancellor to get up private theatricals in one of the dormitories, with no raised stage and no scenery. This scheme gave rise to no end of pleasant excitement and bustle. A curtain, made of sheets sewn together, divided the long dormitory in two; the place for the stage was fenced off by bedsteads and lighted by candlesticks from the classrooms. We acted *Serve Him Right*, a comedy by Veryovkin, and the parts of the old and the young Doblestin were taken by myself and Panayev. The costumes were ludicrous. For instance, old Doblestin wore a tattered military tunic, borrowed from one of our porters who was an old soldier, and a tow wig whitened with chalk; the fetters on his hands were borrowed from a watch-dog, who took advantage of his free evening to bite someone very severely. A student called Perevoshchikov, with a pale and not young face and a hoarse voice, was excellent in the old woman's part, and parts of the kind were always assigned to him afterwards. I and my dog-chain produced a powerful effect: I was hailed as a genius, and so was Peter Zikov, who threw the whole audience into convulsions by his comic powers. But alas! my bosom friend, Panayev, in spite of his good looks, pleased nobody in the part of young Doblestin. He had in fact a rather plaintive and cold delivery, and he was handicapped by a defect in pronunciation, which he could not overcome. This was my first public success as an actor; our acting at the Panayevs' house had been private, and the audience very small, but now all the chief officials were present, the professors and teachers and even their wives and daughters, not to mention as many students and schoolboys as could be crammed into the room.

Soon afterwards the Chancellor sent his permission: a theater might be made for the Government students as "a reward for their exemplary diligence." At the same time the inspector was charged to keep an eye on the pieces chosen, and also to see that this form of amusement did not interfere with serious study. We were all delighted. A stage and background, which could be easily and quickly removed, were put up at the expense of the Government; but the students reduced the cost considerably by painting the scenery themselves. It was intended at first to construct the theater in one of the halls, but this turned out to be uncomfortably large, and the authorities objected to the expense; finally the choice fell on one of the classrooms, which was especially suitable because it was divided in the middle by an arch. There had been two rooms originally, but the dividing wall had been removed some years before, and an arch, resting on two pillars at the side, was left to support the ceiling. For the erection of a stage this was a great convenience. But we were too impatient to wait for the completion of our theater, and played a comedy by Kotzebue, *Misanthropy and Remorse*,* in the hall that I mentioned above. I distinguished myself in the part of The Stranger, and my fame was established on a solid foundation. Next we drew up a code of regulations and confirmed it by the signatures of all who took part in the acting; and I, young as I was, was chosen as manager of the company. But alas! I did not hold this position for long: I gained some distinction in another comedy by Kotzebue, and then an unfortunate combination of circumstances banished me from the stage for a whole year. I must describe in somewhat greater detail this tragi-comic affair.

The next play we took in hand was *Meinau, or The Result of Reconciliation*, written by some German author to express his opinion that the reconciliation between Meinau and his erring wife, which concludes Kotzebue's comedy of *Misanthropy and Remorse*, cannot restore their domestic happiness. The piece included the small part of a General who had once been in love with Meinau's wife: he happens to meet Meinau and his wife, whereupon the lady faints and the husband challenges the General and kills him in a duel with pistols. After his failure as Doblestin, Alexander Panayev had taken little part in our performances, though he was still a member of the company; but when he heard our choice of a play, he begged me to give him the General's part. He admitted that he had no gift for the stage, but he had special reasons for wishing to have this part assigned to him. These reasons I knew: he was attached to a certain young lady who always attended our performances, and

* The English version of this play is known as *The Stranger*.

he wished her to see him on the stage, wearing a general's uniform with large epaulettes, and falling at the fatal shot. Now I knew that the rest of the company would resent my decision; and I knew that another actor, Peter Balyasnikov, whose character and ability gave him a marked ascendancy among us, wished to have this part and would play it ever so much better; but I was led astray by the claims of friendship, and allotted the part to Panayev, which as manager of the company, I had a perfect right to do. The others at once declared that Panayev would ruin the whole play, but I replied that the part was small and unimportant, that Panayev had gone through it with me very well, that I would undertake to make him perfect, and that his good looks gave him a special claim to it. Out of respect for my authority as manager, they submitted, but with much reluctance. But Panayev was such a failure at the first rehearsal that it was painful to me to look at him, and the company attacked me again, begging me to choose anyone but Panayev for the part. I refused, urging for my friend that he did not know the part, and vouching for it that with my coaching he would do very well. But I saw trouble ahead, and privately begged my friend to resign. It was in vain; he begged me with tears not to deprive him of the opportunity to make a favorable impression on the heart of his fair one; he feared a rival, and that rival was Balyasnikov! I was so affected by this appeal that I took an oath not to give the part to anyone else, and I promised, in case of a serious revolt, to resign my own part of Meinau. At the second rehearsal, Panayev, though he knew his part, acted as badly as before. Taking advantage of my powers as manager, I had excluded everybody but the actors from this rehearsal, but during the scene between me and the General, the door opened and I saw Balyasnikov come in with several others. He stopped

right in front of the stage and looked very contemptuous
and insolent. I had hardly killed the General, when all the
company came round me and insisted that I should give the
part to Balyasnikov instead. Panayev turned pale. Eager
in defense of my friend, and insulted in my dignity as manager, I refused positively and used a threat: "You are inter-
fering in what is no business of yours," I said, "and if you
won't obey me, I resign the part of Meinau and decline to
take any further share in the acting."

I expected to cause a sensation by my closing words. My
head had been turned by praise and my high opinion of
myself, till I thought that I was indispensable, but my oppo-
nents were only waiting for the opening I had given them.
Balyasnikov at once stepped forward and made a speech.
He said coolly that I was conceited and thought myself a
great actor, that I misused my power as manager and was
sacrificing the play and the whole company to my friendship for Panayev, who could not act at all. "Our praise gave
you glory," he added, "and we shall also rob you of it, and
assert everywhere that you cannot act. We deprive you of
the management and expel you from the company." The
rest unanimously expressed their agreement. Though I was
expecting a revolt against my authority, I had not foreseen
such a blow as this. I rallied all my presence of mind, took
my friend Panayev by the hand with the fortitude of a hero,
and left the room without saying a word. I returned home
stunned by my fall and also conscious of my unfair deal-
ing, but I tried to comfort myself with the thought that I
had sacrificed my own vanity and passion for the stage to
my friend's peace of mind. I believed that the piece could
not be acted without me and that therefore his hated rival
could not appear in the glittering epaulettes to steal away
the heart of the fair lady. But it was a great blow to Panayev

and me when we went next day to college and heard that the company had elected Balyasnikov manager on the previous evening, that my part had been given to Dmitriev, and that Balyasnikov himself was to act the General.

Dmitriev was a pensioner student of remarkable ability; he had been my regular rival in all our studies, though up till now I had almost always distanced him. In Ibrahimov's class his compositions on the subjects set to us were sometimes as good as mine, and Ibrahimov, in spite of some partiality for me, on two occasions informed the whole class that he could not determine the order of merit between our essays. He had also a reputation for reciting, and I had sometimes seen him declaiming poetry to a crowd of listeners. Speaking candidly, I must admit that Dmitriev had perhaps more talent for literature and the stage than I had, but, as neither the one nor the other inspired in him the exclusive passion that I felt, his gifts were unimproved and undeveloped. Also, in his appearance, which was rather rough and uncouth, and in all his movements, there was visible a certain heaviness and a want of ease and grace. It never entered my head that such a savage would consent to appear on the stage, but the company appealed to him and induced him with some difficulty to take the part of Meinau. They gave him the book and made him read the part aloud on the spot, and were delighted one and all by his performance. We were told that many of his audience were reduced to tears and that a student called Chesnov, a bosom friend of Dmitriev's and a great laugher and good-humored joker, had shed floods of tears. To me and my friend this was absolute death and destruction: what had become of his love affair and my vanity and passion for the stage? If I had acted justly and assigned the General's part to someone else, Balyasnikov would never have got the part or the chance to appear in the glittering epaulettes! The play was at last performed, and Panayev and I were a little consoled because it was not a great success. Neither of us was present, and my report of its failure depends on the general verdict of the teachers and unprejudiced spectators, though the students and especially the actors were loud in their praise of Dmitriev. Having seen him at a rehearsal, I am myself convinced that he was very good in the striking passages of the part, if not in all.

Torn from the stage by this combination of circumstances, I next dashed off in a different direction, towards literature and natural history. On the latter subject I attended lectures given in French by Professor Fuchs, and I became interested chiefly in collecting butterflies, which soon was an absorbing passion with me. Panayev was my faithful companion and collaborator in the whole business. We spent all our leisure in wandering, nets in hand, through gardens and meadows and woods, and chasing all the butterflies we came across; the moths we searched for under boughs and leaves, in hollow trees, or in the chinks of fences and stone walls.

I went to lectures in college and kept up my attendance at two classes in the school, and my progress was fairly satisfactory, but not more. I began a course on anatomy with much interest and enjoyed the lectures, as long as the dissection was confined to animals, living or dead. I was even thought likely to do well in the subject, but, when it came to the dissection of corpses, I gave up anatomy for good. I was afraid of dead bodies. But my companions felt quite differently: they ransacked the town for a "subject," and, when one was found and brought to the anatomical school, they hailed it with joyful triumph. For long I was unable to look at some of *them* without disgust.

In describing my dramatic career, I have run on far ahead, and now I must go back and give an account of my life with my tutor, Kartashevsky, and of some changes that had taken place. When we acted for the first time, by day and in the Panayevs' house, my tutor knew nothing of it; but when we determined to start a theater in the college and I told him of this, he raised no obstacle to my taking part in the scheme, and even expressed approval. Later, when he saw the comedy *Serve Him Right*, he was pleased with my acting and laughed a great deal at my costume. I must confess that the theater monopolized my attention far too much, but it is also true that my tutor began to pay less attention to me. I do not know the original cause of this change, and I should be glad if I could clear it up in my own mind. It is true that some trifling differences gave rise for a time to a certain coldness between us; yet I do not believe that they could have led to such serious and unexpected consequences, except by the evil influence of some third party.

Our first difference was caused by his discovering in my possession two novels that he had prohibited—*The Boy by the Stream* by Kotzebue, and *Nature and Love* by Auguste La Fontaine. I used to read them at night or in the unused rooms, and they gave me an ecstasy of delight. It sounds absurd, but even now the words, "Love me, Fanny; I am kind," or "Months, blissful months flew by over these happy mortals"*—trifling and silly as the words are in themselves —make my heart beat faster, at the mere recollection of that intense delight which they gave to the boy of fifteen. The fact is that the words do not matter: all depends upon the feeling which the reader brings to them. I was certainly to blame, but my tutor censured my fault too severely, and if

* The quotations are from *Nature and Love.*

I had believed what he said, I should have been in despair. But I could not admit that I was so great a criminal, and so it became possible and reasonable for me to accuse my tutor of injustice and want of consideration towards me. On this occasion, however, our friendly relations were restored pretty soon.

Our second difference arose as follows. On the day before Trinity Sunday, my tutor decided to take me to Zapolsky's country house for the weekend. But this time I did not wish to leave Kazan, because Panayev and I had made a toy theater, with elaborate scenery. It had ingenious devices for changing the scenes, and one of the scenes was a storm with thunder and lightning; Panayev was a great hand at all contrivances of this kind. As a performance had been fixed for the Monday and an audience invited, it was vexing to me to be absent, but I submitted without grumbling. On the day fixed for our departure, I asked leave of my tutor to spend some hours at Panayev's house. He consented, but said that if I did not return by seven o'clock he would start alone; I promised to return without fail. Panayev and I put our toy theater through a "dress rehearsal," but some of the phenomena would not come right: the lightning missed the tree which it was bound to strike and set fire to, the moon refused to appear from behind the clouds, and the waterfall ceased at times to fall. I was so much taken up in regulating these natural phenomena that I did not notice when my time was up. When I became aware of this, I ran all the way home, but still I was a quarter of an hour late. My tutor had started alone exactly at seven; he was very angry and had left no directions for me. In what followed I was really to blame: though Yevseich proposed that we should hire horses and follow at once, I refused flatly to do so. I said that Kartashevsky might have waited for me or left instructions for me to come on alone. I went back to the Panayevs' house and spent the whole night in working at the puppet show. Alarmed by my long absence, Yevseich came for me himself. We showed him the theater, and he was not a little surprised by our cleverness; I went home with him at sunrise. Again he urged me to join my tutor in the country, and again I flatly refused. On Trinity Sunday Panayev dined at my house, and after dinner we went off to the park, which was close by and a regular resort for a great concourse of people at Whitsuntide. Next day the performance took place at the Panayevs' house and was a splendid success: the oak was shattered and burnt by the lightning, the moon duly rose from behind the clouds, the waterfall foamed and splashed without stopping. The hosts and the spectators alike were delighted, but I felt as if cats were scratching at my heart.

Early on Tuesday my tutor returned. While I was still in bed, he had a stormy interview with Yevseich, who told him all that had happened, not even keeping back that he had twice over proposed to me to follow. My tutor refused to see me, and for forty-eight hours we did not meet, even for dinner. I was greatly distressed, but I also felt injured: I was nearly sixteen, and I felt that such treatment was unreasonable except in the case of a boy. The explanation came at last. I had prepared myself to face it firmly and coolly, and was able at first to meet and parry all his harsh rebukes with an appearance of calmness; but when he said, "Now, what will be your mother's feeling when I describe your conduct and refuse to go on living with you any longer?"—then my firmness melted like wax, tears gushed from my eyes, I confessed myself entirely in the wrong and sincerely begged his forgiveness of my fault. But now Kartashevsky made a great mistake: instead of catching at my sincere repentance, he met it coldly and refused to make it up with me entirely. Perhaps he did not quite believe me, but it is more likely that he acted thus from calculation: he knew that my mind was too quick in losing the impressions which it was too quick in receiving, and wished by a change in his behavior to make me feel my fault more deeply. But the result was not in the least what he expected. While changing towards me, he expected me to remain the same; but to my nature these cold relations were intolerable, and I soon began to think myself always in the right and he in the wrong, and my attachment to him was shaken.

At last an utterly trifling incident finally changed the former relations between us. The Bursar, Markevich, died. I have said already that he always showed kindness to me and that I was much attached to him. But I had been afraid from childhood of the sight of a dead body, and therefore, in spite of the arguments and remonstrances of my tutor, I positively refused to attend the funeral. Kartashevsky came back from the sad ceremony and brought with him Chekiev, the teacher of drawing. I ought first to say that I had a strong dislike for this gentleman, who was a great fop and annoyed me by his silly jokes. It was always a surprise to me that my tutor could be on intimate terms with such a fool, but the simple explanation was that they had been schoolfellows together at Moscow. On this day Chekiev was more troublesome than usual: Why had I not been at the funeral? Why had I not paid the last tribute of respect to one who was so fond of me? He declared that my conduct proved the hardness of my heart, and so on. In a word, he teased me beyond bounds. When he said with a sneer, "Confess that you are really not at all afraid of dead bodies, and that this fear is merely a selfish pretence," I grew very angry and answered roughly and rudely, "You are quite right. My fear of dead bodies is a mere sham." Now that I consider these words coolly, I do not see in them the importance that my tutor attached to them. His features changed with displeasure, and he said in a low but significant voice, "After the language which you have ventured to address in my presence to my friend and guest, you can judge yourself whether we are likely to be agreeable to one another. Please go to your own room." Not feeling myself to blame, I was naturally angrier than ever, but I left the room without a word. This took place just before dinner, when the meal was already on the table. Yevseich came after me with my knife and fork and napkin; he explained that my tutor ordered me to dine in my room. This redoubled my fury, and nothing but the thought of my mother kept me from going straight to my tutor and pouring out a torrent of abuse. I must do justice to Chekiev: he went on for a long time begging Kartashevsky to pardon me, but with no effect. This I was told by Yevseich. After dinner Chekiev came to my door, but I locked myself in and would not admit him. Next day my tutor summoned me and said coldly and firmly, "We cannot go on living together, and I must resign my position as your tutor; but we must both try to lighten as much as possible the blow which our separation will inflict on your mother, and we must manage this business without insulting one another." I answered that he had anticipated my wish and that I had intended to make exactly the same suggestion to him. "Then that is all right," he said with a sneer, and nodded to me to go. I went off to my room and gave myself up in my solitude to excitement and anger. I thought myself entirely in the right and my tutor entirely in the wrong.

And here I must confess to an action that is difficult to excuse on the ground of irritation and impulsiveness. Unluckily, the following day was post day, and I wrote a long letter to my parents in which I showed no mercy to my tutor and spoke of him in language so insulting that I blush for it now. If I had put off writing till next post, I should have thought better of it, beyond doubt, but then, and often afterwards throughout my life, I was carried away by my impetuous nature. Next day, when the letter had gone, my conscience began to reproach me, and I kept constantly thinking of my tutor's words, that we ought not to insult each other. But what were my feelings, when, after some days during which we met only at dinner and hardly spoke, my tutor summoned me and read over to me a very long letter that he had ready to send to my mother! This letter was full of good sense and affectionate feeling: he confessed himself entirely unfit to go on acting as tutor and director to a young man who could no longer be treated as a boy and needed something different. He declared that he had no idea how to tackle such a problem; he felt that he was mismanaging it and might in this way do me harm. Then he described in detail my intellect and character and my tastes, and foretold their future development; he also described my defects; but the bright side with its happy promise for the future was thrown into relief, and he spoke indulgently of my failings, and said that time and experience would root them out. He vouched for my good principles; it would be quite safe, he said, for me to live alone or with a friend, Alexander Panayev for instance, or with some professor, not as a pupil but as a young friend. It was even desirable that I should be my own master for a year or so before entering on a profession; it would be bad for me to pass directly from the control of a strict tutor to independence and a career divided between society and professional occupations. He ended by saying that he intended soon to leave Kazan for Petersburg, in order to take steps towards getting a post in the teaching profession there or possibly in the civil service.

The effect produced on me by this letter was positively alarming to my tutor. Conscience-stricken and repentant, I was so agitated that for long I could not speak a word. Tears at last relieved the burden on my heart, and I made a clean breast of my letter home, expressed all my old feeling of attachment, and begged and prayed him with tears to forget what I had done, and not to part with me till he went to Petersburg. I promised—and I should certainly have kept the promise—that, however severely he might treat me, I should not feel it, far less resent it. The sincerity of my repentance and distress seemed to shake his determination. He looked at me long and attentively, and then began to walk about the room; at last he said, "This needs thinking over," and let me go. Two days remained before the next post went. I wrote another letter to my parents, in which I confessed that I was entirely to blame and had sinned beyond forgiveness; I praised my tutor enthusiastically, described the whole affair in detail, and ended by saying, "However Kartashevsky treats me—whether he lets me stay or drives me from him—I shall continue to love him as a second father." Before I sent off the letter, I took it to my tutor and asked if he wished to read it. He refused, saying that he had already sent off the letter I had heard, and that the matter was definitely settled. To me this was a blow; I cannot say that it was quite unexpected, but it was heavy all the same. I knew that no attacks would make my tutor withdraw from his position, and any withdrawal would have been useless, because his letter was already posted. There was nothing to be done, and I made haste to send off my own letter.

The picture that my lively imagination painted of my mother's despair followed me day and night till grief made me ill. Kartashevsky frowned at this. He disapproved of all my fits of excitement, and pointed out the obvious danger of uncontrolled feeling in any direction; but at the same time he pitied me and tried to comfort me by saying that my mother would take it much more coolly than I imagined, that our parting was inevitable in any case, and that my second letter—I had repeated its contents to him—would wipe out the painful impression left by its predecessor. I took some comfort from his words and soon got well, and before long letters arrived from Aksakovo, which entirely confirmed my tutor's opinion. My father and mother appreciated my repentance and forgave me for the first letter, written as it was in a fit of anger. My mother put entire confidence in my tutor's report about me, and her loving heart was filled with bright and happy hopes for the future. She believed him also when he said that private affairs made it necessary for him to leave Kazan without delay. She was convinced that he would always be a true friend of the family, that after ceasing to be my tutor, he would draw closer to me and like me better, and that I should take his advice with more readiness and more in earnest when it came unaccompanied by any flavor of authority. Nor was she mistaken: the future confirmed the anticipations of her rare intelligence.

My summer holidays were now approaching. Kartashevsky intended to leave for Petersburg in another month, and my mother asked him to make arrangements for my future residence at Kazan. With his consent—I am surprised that he gave it—I arranged with Levitsky, the assistant professor of Philosophy and Logic, that I should live in his house, paying a small sum for board and lodging and also looking after his three pupils who were pensioners in the school. All three boys were as old as I, and great scamps, though I had no idea of this at the time. I parted with Kartashevsky with much feeling and even wept; he was much moved himself, but tried as usual to hide his feeling by jesting and even making fun of my sensibility.

In spite of the confusion and unrest that troubled my life at this time in my tutor's house, Panayev and I continued to interest ourselves in literature and to collect butterflies; my friend was very neat and skillful with his hands and could set butterflies to perfection. I wrote several poems and a prose article entitled *Friendship*, and showed them to my friend. He approved of them, but made some criticisms that seemed to me unfounded. I shall insert here my first childish verses, of which, however, I have forgotten half; and thus I celebrate my jubilee after fifty years spent in spoiling paper. I should add that I had no cruel charmer; in fact I was not acquainted with any young lady.

To a Nightingale

O friend of Spring, dearest of songsters,
Be thou alone my comfort!
Lighten the cruel pain
That devours my passionate heart.

Sing the charms of my loved one,
Sing my fiery love for her,
Recount all my sufferings,
Recount my days of mourning.

Let her hear thy voice,
Let her know who taught thee!
It may be, the hardhearted one
For pity's sake will sigh for me.

It may be, she will learn from thee
That love for man is happiness;
It may be, she will feel at last
That life without love is misery.
(Several stanzas are wanting.)

Such were the unrhymed verses with which I made my appearance on the literary stage, while I was still a boy at school in the year 1805. But I soon considered these verses "unworthy of my pen," and did not give them a place in our magazine of 1806. All my subsequent poems were in rhyme, and they are all completely devoid of any merit, even if allowances be made; they show not the smallest sign of a gift for poetry.

I spent the summer vacation of 1805 at Aksakovo, and somehow I remember little about it, except that I was keenly interested in shooting and butterflies; I seldom fished, probably because the larger fish do not take freely at that season.

I found my mother in a bad state of health, and learned that this was the only reason that prevented her from setting out for Kazan when she heard of the breach between me and Kartashevsky. I still confided everything to her without reserve, and when I had told her all the minutest particulars of my life and even my thoughts, she felt happy about me. In spite of my youth, she let me go back to Kazan to live with a professor about whom she knew nothing, fully believing in the steadiness of my principles and the blamelessness of my conduct.

On returning to Kazan, I went straight to Levitsky's house. Not long before my return, Kartashevsky had left for Petersburg, and I was much surprised to hear that he had spent a whole month of the vacation in idleness at Kazan. Until a new professor was appointed, the teaching of higher mathematics was entrusted to a student, Alexander Knyazhevich, whose remarkable powers gave promise of a distinguished career in that branch of learning.* It was impossible for me to stay long with Levitsky. A fatal passion for drink had completely mastered him, and at this time he shut himself up every evening to gratify it; his pupils were absolutely free to do as they liked and learned nothing at all. I soon grew tired of looking after these young scapegraces, and, with my parents' consent, I parted from Levitsky at the end of two months and took lodgings in the house of a German named Hermann, near the theater. Here I settled down by myself and began for the first time to live alone and uncontrolled. Panayev and I were almost inseparable, and we took another student, D. Perevoshchikov,† into our literary partnership. We translated tales by Marmontel, those which Karamzin had not translated; we wrote original poetry and prose, and each read his translations and compositions to the other two. I had planned to translate Marmontel before I left Levitsky, and I told him so one day, before dinner, of course, while he was still sober; and I clearly remember how insulted I was by his reply: "Translate Marmontel after Karamzin! You are a bold man, but 'fools rush in where angels fear to tread.'" But these words did not stop us. At last Panayev and I determined to publish a magazine in manuscript in the coming year of 1806; it was to be called *A Journal of our Occupations*, and no editor's name was to appear. This was a more serious undertaking than *Shepherds of Arcadia*, and I did all I could to keep out of this magazine all mechanical imitation of Karamzin, and to discourage the predilection of my friend for pastoral writ-

* He became Minister of Finance in the Russian Government.

† Afterwards famous as a mathematician and astronomer.

ing. Against the former I was struggling at this time with all my might, and I found support in a book by Shishkov,* *A Discussion of the Old and New Styles*, which carried me to the opposite extreme. I shall speak of this in more detail elsewhere. I have preserved three numbers of our magazine, and I see that it began in April and appeared for the last time in December. These numbers do not contain a single article, original or translated, from my pen, though I remember that I wrote many; I am sorry, because it would interest me now to see how I expressed my literary creed of those days.

Meantime, at the end of 1805 and in the following January, the students twice acted plays without my taking part in them. This deprivation was a bitter pill to me; my love for acting was ungratified, and my vanity was hurt by the success of my rival, Dmitriev, but there was nothing to be done. The actors proposed that I should rejoin the company, but I had not yet forgotten their insulting treatment of me, and my reply was, "You don't want me, you have got Dmitriev who plays my parts excellently." "Well, just as you choose! Sulk, if you like! We can get on without you," said Balyasnikov the manager; and there the matter ended. There was no ill-feeling, however: I attended rehearsals and gave my advice to any who asked it. The first performance was Kotzebue's comedy *Misanthropy and Remorse*; Dmitriev played The Stranger with great success. He had, indeed, no idea how to hold himself; his attitudes were absurd, and his gestures still more so, because he used his right hand only while his left remained as if tied behind his back; and in

* Aksakov wrote a very entertaining account of his acquaintance with Shishkov at Petersburg in later years. Shishkov, an admiral and high official, was also an ardent upholder of archaic style. In private life he was the most absent-minded and most disinterested of men.

ordinary conversation with his servant and the old villager, his acting was positively bad. Yet in the scene with the friend to whom he tells his misfortunes and in the reconciliation with his wife, Dmitriev showed such power of feeling that all the spectators, myself included, were quite carried away and expressed their delight by frantic applause. At first, I felt nothing but delight, and no trace of jealousy had stolen into my heart; but afterwards I was deeply wounded by some remarks of the students, especially the actors, and then the green-eyed monster took up its abode in my breast. They said very rudely, "You see, we got on all right without you. You could never play The Stranger like Dmitriev. The people who praised *you* had never seen *him*." It was true that his success in the part had been much more brilliant than mine, and yet I had a few partisans who maintained that my performance was better, and that Dmitriev caricatured the part, succeeding only in a few striking passages. I, they said, was a real actor and did justice to the part from beginning to end, from the first word to the last. This was partly true, and I conceived an intense desire to study the part of The Stranger and then to act it in such a way as totally to eclipse my rival.

At the beginning of 1806 the students gave a second performance in which they acted another play by Kotzebue, *Poverty and Honor*; Dmitriev took the part of Heinrich Blum, and scored another success, though it was not so great a success as The Stranger. My champions declared that I would have been beyond comparison better as Heinrich Blum. Spurred on by jealousy and vanity, I worked up both these parts with great care and then recited them, or rather acted the striking passages of both, before a large audience of students. They were not all predisposed to favor me, but they all felt the difference between me and my rival, between his powerful but uncouth expression of feeling and my more polished and natural acting. And now two parties of equal strength arose among the students, one for me and the other against; and this was my first step on the way to triumph. There were noisy disputes, which led on to quarrels and all but ended in blows. This was some consolation to my vanity, and before long a sudden turn made me the spoiled child of fortune. Dmitriev, who was now over twenty, became discontented with the instruction given by the professors, which, to tell the truth, was very unsatisfactory. There may have been other reasons as well—I do not know; anyhow, he decided to enter the Army and left the University at short notice; being a good mathematician, he chose the artillery. The bereaved company was forced to appeal to me for aid. Taking advantage of the position, I would not consent for a long time, though they offered to reappoint me as manager. At last, when I had coquetted long enough, I agreed, on two conditions: (1) the title and office of manager were to be abolished, and a committee of three to be elected to manage the company; (2) our performances were to begin with a repetition of the two plays, *Misanthropy and Remorse* and *Poverty and Honor*. As a matter of course, they all agreed to my conditions.

The former play was performed in Easter week. Gruzinov, an actor at the Kazan theater for whom we all had much liking and respect, came somehow to be invited to the dress rehearsal. The piece had been acted by the students twice before; we all worked hard, I harder than anyone, and the result was fairly successful. Gruzinov was astonished; he could not believe his own eyes and ears. He praised us so highly that Yesipov, the manager of the town theater, bestirred himself to get Yakovkin's permission to attend the actual performance, and not only came himself but brought with him four actors, of whom Gruzinov was one. At last I had the opportunity that I had so long desired and looked forward to. My youthful vanity was satisfied: all the students said that I had excelled myself and quite distanced Dmitriev. What more could I wish? Alas for the transitory nature of earthly glory! But two or three months had passed since the triumph of Dmitriev; now only one or two partisans were left, who said in whispers that Dmitriev acted the part not worse than Aksakov, and some passages better; and this was perfectly true. A good many strangers saw the play, and they praised me to the skies, but my glory derived its chief brilliance and permanence from the praise of Yesipov and his actors, whose verdict was with justice considered to carry weight. In the other play, *Poverty and Honor*, which had been acted already early in the year, I hoped to win a still greater triumph, and the reader will see presently that I was not disappointed.

I must now go back in my narrative. Kartashevsky, owing to his long delay in Kazan, outstayed his leave of absence and was more than a month late in returning. He did not present any medical certificate or state any urgent reasons that might have justified or at least excused his absence. The University authorities were displeased at his conduct and passed a vote of censure at their council: they fined him and entered on his certificate the fact of his absence without leave. He was offended and asked leave to resign his post. After some delay, he was allowed to resign, but it was resolved to enter his offense and punishment on his leaving certificate. He refused to accept such a certificate, left the place, and entered the public service at Petersburg without any certificate; the department he joined was the Legislative Commission. After a long time and much trouble, he procured an order from the Minister of Education that the

University should issue a certificate without the objectionable particulars. I often saw my former tutor before he left
Kazan, and I felt at parting that he was a kind friend older
than myself, whom I had to thank for the purity of my ideals
and convictions. What my mother had foretold was beginning to come true.

In the year 1806 another event took place, the importance
of which was long unrealized by me, though its consequences
entirely changed the position of my family. Praskovya Ivanovna Kurolyesova died, after suffering for nearly a year
from dropsy. During all this time my parents lived at Old
Aksakovo with their other children; I mean, that the children lived at Aksakovo, while my father and mother never
left the sufferer who was at Chufarovo; but when she was
removed to Simbirsk, our whole family went there too. Praskovya Ivanovna was a remarkable woman: she bore her
grievous illness with astonishing patience, calmness, and
even cheerfulness, and she face death with a degree of fortitude of which few are capable. She had twice been tapped
for dropsy; when the operation had been performed a third
time, her doctor, a Jew, looked at the wounds, and expressed
much satisfaction with the result. "None of your lies!" said
the patient. "I can see that the end is coming. There is a
great change in me, and that is erysipelas on my skin. I do
not fear death; I got ready for it long ago. But tell me, thou
seed of Jacob, how long I have to live." The doctor, though
he was accustomed to be addressed in this fashion, never
failed to resent it. He answered in relentless tones, "You
will live four days more." "Thank you for telling the truth,"
answered the patient, and this time she spoke quite politely.
"Now good-bye! I thank you for your trouble and beg you
not to come again. I shall order your fees to be paid at once."
Then she assembled the entire household, and announced

that she was dying; she refused any further treatment and asked to be left in peace; no one was to stay in the room, except one person to read the Gospel aloud. She turned to my father and asked, "Have I done all that ought to be done? Is nothing more needed?" "Nothing, aunt," he replied. "You settled everything long ago." "Well, that is all right," said the patient. "I wish no one to be distressed about me. Now, please leave the room."

Praskovya Ivanovna lived on for five days. She spent the whole of that time in repeating prayers, or singing part of the Church service, or listening while the Gospel was read. About worldly affairs she did not speak a single word to anyone. By her desire, all took farewell of her in silence, and she spoke just four parting words to each member of the household, even to her hall-porter—"Forgive me, a sinner!" I heard of all this by letters from my family, but they told me nothing more. Before long, I heard that I had a third sister, and that, though my mother had been desperately ill, all was now going on well. I was alarmed at first, but then took courage, and further letters set my mind completely at rest on the score of my mother's health.

Panayev and I went on zealously with the old occupations —working at literature, visiting the theater, and collecting butterflies when the spring came on. I must confess with shame that, apart from these hobbies, I was idle enough and that my distractions from study were frequent and absorbing.

Among these distractions I may reckon the formation of a small Literary Club, with Ibrahimov as president. The founders and original members were Ibrahimov, Bogdanov, a teacher in the school, and six students, including Panayev and myself. We met every Saturday to read our compositions and translations in verse and prose. Every member had the right of criticism, and the articles were sometimes corrected on the spot, if the author admitted the justice of the improvements suggested; there was never any quarrelling. If any piece was accepted, it was copied out in a book that we started for the purpose. After I left Kazan, the membership was increased and bylaws drawn up; finally "The Society of Lovers of Russian Literature at Kazan University" was formally opened by permission of the Imperial Government. It still exists but, like all our Literary Societies, in a state of suspended animation. I have still the distinction of ranking as an honorary member.

There happened about this time at Kazan a remarkable incident in which I was directly concerned. A private school for boys and girls was kept in the town by a German couple, by the name of Wilfing. Having no children of their own, they had adopted a destitute orphan, Marya Kermik, who was now grown up and very pretty. Kartashevsky sometimes called on the Wilfings and took me there twice, but, at the time I am speaking of, I had not been there for more than six months. A chance meeting in the course of a jaunt out of the town renewed our acquaintance, and the girl's beauty soon asserted its influence over me. I naturally revealed my secret to my bosom friend, Panayev. He was delighted, embraced me warmly, and congratulated me on "beginning to live." He used every effort to fan the spark that had dropped upon my youthful heart. As Marya was a very quiet, modest girl, all her many admirers sighed for her at a respectful distance; and of my feelings she had of course no idea. Visionary hopes and visionary disappointments, which I expressed in wretched boyish verses, were still going on when suddenly a mysterious traveler, a Swedish Count, turned up at Kazan for a short stay. He made the acquaintance of the Wilfings and charmed them all;

he went there daily and spent the whole day at their house. He was a handsome man of about thirty-five, clever, pleasant, and lively, a skillful artist and a master of many languages, and an author as well both in verse and prose. In three days, the Wilfings were raving about him; in a week Marya had fallen in love with him; and, at the end of another fortnight, he married her and carried her off with him to Siberia, where he had been sent by the Government to conduct some scientific investigation, with an official to act as interpreter, because the Count himself did not understand a word of Russian. The Wilfings found it hard to part with their adopted daughter, whom they loved as if she had been their own; but they did not venture to complain of the match, which seemed so enviable, so astonishing, and so dazzling. She was a baker's daughter, and she had married a Count, who adored his wife and was richly endowed with every gift of nature and education. People less simple than the Wilfings might easily have been seduced by an event so wonderful.

But alas, the riddle was soon explained! The Count had conferred this title on himself; he was a notorious swindler and adventurer, well known for his exploits in Germany under the name of Aschenbrenner. From Germany he had fled to Russia for fear of the police; he became a Russian subject and spent several years in the western provinces, where he was implicated in many frauds and finally banished to Siberia. The official who accompanied him was a police officer with a German name whose business it was to convey his charge incognito to Irkutsk, and hand him over personally to the governor there for rigorous supervision. But all these facts were somehow kept from the public and from the Wilfings. The traveler had no need of an interpreter, for it was afterwards discovered that he spoke Russian very well. In the course of his journey he himself wrote to the Wilfings and informed them of the imposture; he said he had been driven to it by the irresistible power of love; of course he called himself the victim of calumny, and hoped to be cleared and compensated for his undeserved sufferings. His wife wrote too; she said that, though she knew all, she still thanked God for her happiness. Later, someone sent to the Wilfings a German work in two volumes, which contained a narrative of the sham Count's adventures written by himself. The man was the Vidocq* of his time. The old Wilfings were inconsolable. I never could find out what was Marya's ultimate fate. Such was the sorrowful ending of my first love story.

For the summer vacation, I went again to Old Aksakovo, where my family then was. I arrived late in the evening, when everyone was in bed; but my mother expected me on that day and, when she heard the sound of my arrival, came out to meet me on the steps and took me straight to her bedroom, where I embraced both my parents and found much to tell and many questions to ask. Then I went to sleep on the sofa in their room. When I awoke rather late, I overheard my parents talking in subdued voices of some business which was a mystery to me. Then my mother noticed that I was not asleep, and said in a low voice to my father, "We must tell Seryozha the whole story; of course he is still quite in the dark." "Do, my dear," said my father. "Are you awake, Seryozha?" "Yes, mother," I answered. "Then come here beside us. We must tell you of something that has happened to us. We have become rich." I got off the sofa and sat down on their bed, and they told me fully and in minute detail what I shall try to convey in a few words.

* Francois Vidocq (1775–1857), a French thief-turned-police-detective, published his own *Memoirs* in 1828.

When Praskovya Ivanovna suddenly became seriously ill of dropsy, she lost no time in making my father the legal heir to all her property, real and personal. The whole affair was settled in the course of a few days; all the district judges traveled to Chufarovo for the purpose, and some persons of credit in the town came as witnesses. In the presence of them all Praskovya Ivanovna signed the necessary documents and confirmed them by a verbal declaration. When all was done, she ordered champagne to be served, took a glass herself, and proposed the health of her heir in cheerful terms. I ought to say that she was dangerously ill at the time and that the doctor who had been summoned at once from Simbirsk, the best doctor at that time, and a Jew, had no hope of her recovery. He determined to relieve her by tapping, though he would not for a moment guarantee the result of the operation; but she retained so much natural force that she soon conquered the disease and was perfectly well in a very short time. Unfortunately Praskovya Ivanovna did not believe in the danger of chills and regarded diet as a mere whimsy of doctors. She resumed her former life and caught a chill, which was followed by indigestion and a return of dropsy. A second operation was less successful and only postponed the fatal event. The patient was taken to Simbirsk, where after a third operation she died; but of this I have spoken already.

Our accession to wealth had surprising results: it was sand in the eyes to people in general, and it raised a ferment of envy in the breasts of near friends and even of relations.

Praskovya Ivanovna had sundry poor debtors. When she was reminded of this on her deathbed, she said that her money was not stolen or ill-gotten, and she did not intend to give it away. My parents, however, forgave debts of this kind to the amount of 20,000 rubles, and gave the debtors to understand that Praskovya Ivanovna had changed her mind and wished them not to be worried for payment. But this generosity disarmed no enemy and earned no gratitude for people who had inherited wealth; and my parents, much mortified, went off after a few months to Aksakovo, intending to live there.

I can honestly say that change of fortune produced no impression at all upon me. I spent the whole vacation partly in shooting, partly in studying plays. When I went back to Kazan, I was just the same thoughtless and far from wealthy student that I had been before, and for a long time I forgot even to tell my bosom friend, Panayev, of the fortunate change in our circumstances. But in my family I noticed a change. There was some talk of going to Kazan for the winter; a letter was sent to Moscow, asking an old friend there to engage a French woman as governess to my sisters; and there was even a plan of going ourselves to Moscow for the following winter, and to Petersburg in the summer, that I might enter some department of the civil service. In order to carry out this last plan, it was settled that I should leave college in the following year, 1807. To all this I listened with tolerable indifference: I felt no vocation at all for the civil service and no desire to go to Petersburg. I even thought it was all mere talk and speculation, but I was mistaken. A month after I returned to Kazan, I got a letter from my father, telling me to make inquiries and take a large house, with comfortable accommodation for all our family and separate rooms as well for two half-sisters of my mother's, who had lived till then at Kazan with other relations. My mother added that, as she intended to go into society on their account, she must make acquaintance with the best people in the town. I was very glad, both on my own account and for my aunts, whom I met fairly often and was really fond of. Without delay I took a large stone house, belonging to a merchant named Komarov, and moved into it myself; I occupied one snug room on the first floor and waited for family to arrive.

In the University, life went on as before. There were four new professors, two of them Germans. The Russians were Kamensky, an assistant professor in the department of medicine, a man of remarkable eloquence, and Gorodchaninov, a teacher of small capacity and old-fashioned ideas, who lectured on Russian Literature. (I forgot to say that his predecessor, poor Levitsky, died of dropsy due to his excesses and was sincerely missed by us all.) At his opening lecture Gorodchaninov began with a silly pompous greeting to his audience, and then, in order to improve his acquaintance with us, proposed that each of us should name the Russian author he liked best and also his favorite passage from that author. As such a question is difficult to answer on the spur of the moment, each of us gave whatever answer came into his head. Many named Karamzin, but the professor frowned and expressed his regret at finding the atmosphere of a University infected by so dangerous a writer. My neighbor then whispered to me, "Watch me, Aksakov, playing up to the old gentleman!"—and when his turn came, he actually got up and said in a loud voice, "Of all writers, I prefer Sumarokov, and I rank highest of all his poetry the dying words of Dmitri the Usurper in the famous tragedy of that name:

Go down to Hell, my soul, to lie in chains for aye!

Then he pretended to stab himself with a roll of paper, and added the following line:

I would that all mankind might share my fate this day!

The students could hardly help laughing, but the professor was so delighted that he jumped down from his raised platform, called my friend up, shook hands with him, and expressed a desire for their better acquaintance. Thereupon he observed that no literature in the world could show a more powerful verse than the second of these. My turn came next. I said that Lomonosov was my favorite author, and that among all his writings I preferred the "Ode from *Job*." The professor's face shone with satisfaction. "May I trouble you to repeat something from that noble poem?" he said. This was exactly what I wanted, for I hoped to petrify the professor by my reciting. But fate punished me cruelly for my vanity and my love of bygone writers. I meant to begin with two famous lines by Lomonosov—

> *O man, who vainly in thy sorrow*
> *Dost murmur at the will of God—*

but with incredible carelessness I came out with a familiar parody of the verses instead. "My dear sir!" cried out the professor, "that is a shocking travesty of the noble poem!" I blushed with confusion, tried again at once, and repeated my mistake! The whole room burst into a roar of laughter; I could not understand how I had done such a thing; I was burning with shame and stupefied with annoyance and confusion. The professor contemptuously told me to sit down and went on questioning the other students. The lecture lasted two hours, and I seemed to sit on hot coals the whole time. At the end I had an interview with the professor and tried to convince him that my unlucky mistake was an accident and a surprise to myself; I had heard the accursed parody twice and had repeated it once myself just before his lecture, and this was the result. I proved to him that I really knew Lomonosov by heart and had named him as my favorite from personal conviction. When he learned further that I was an admirer of Shishkov, he soon made friends with me, being himself a passionate "Shishkovite." Thus I had put myself right in the eyes of the professor, but I could not escape from the banter of my companions, which went on till they were tired of it. They laughed less at my mistake than at the similarity of taste between me and the professor. For several days running, a number of them greeted me with low bows and congratulated me on having found a kindred spirit, by which they meant a worshipper of Shishkov and an opponent of Karamzin's innovations; each asked me, "How is your friend and patron, Gorodchaninov? When did you last see him? When will you see him again?"—and so on. Their mockery annoyed me, but quarrelling did no good and patience was the only remedy.

Meantime the play, which I had settled on long before, and in which I hoped to score a final triumph over my rival Dmitriev, was getting into shape; it was Kotzebue's *Poverty and Honor.* We invited the actor, Gruzinov, to two rehearsals, and though he now and then stopped the others and suggested improvements, he passed no criticisms on my acting, only saying from time to time, "Very good! Excellent!" At last the play was acted, and brilliant success crowned my hopes: there was not one admirer of Dmitriev's who was not obliged to admit that I had played the part of Heinrich Blum infinitely better. The manager of the Kazan theater gave me a free ticket of admission for every performance. This was the last piece in which I acted at college, my last stage triumph at Kazan. I am not ashamed to say that the recollection of it still awakens pleasant echoes in my breast. There is a fascination which is difficult to explain, in arousing the enthusiasm of an audience. To move a crowd of spectators, to dominate their minds, to compel them to share the feelings which you are expressing and to live your life for the moment—this is a pleasure that fills the actor's heart for long and can never be forgotten.

There was another play, *The Robbers* by Schiller, which we had long intended to act, and all the company and the other students were ardently desirous to have it performed, but the thing dragged on, because the enterprise was difficult and beyond our powers. I was not very eager about it myself, for I attached much importance to the general effect of each performance, and we had no good actors to take the principal parts, those of Karl and Franz Moor. At last a Karl was found in a young man who had never appeared on a stage before; his name was Vasfliev, and he was then a teacher in the school. His reading of the part delighted everyone except me. The students were very fond of him, as he had been a popular boy at school, and they were attracted by his appearance, especially his expressive face, flashing black eyes, and fine voice. But I thought him deficient in art, and also that he did not possess that fire which nothing can take the place of—that visionary reckless passion which alone can give meaning and character to the part of Karl Moor. Our Franz Moor was positively bad. I took the part of the old Count, their father. We rehearsed the play to the best of our ability and intended to perform it Christmas week. My family had now been at Kazan for some time, and I was pleased to think that they would see me act, and particularly anxious to be seen by that dear friend, my pretty young sister; but just a week before the date of the performance, an order was received from a very high quarter, forbidding us to act *The Robbers*.

My family had come to Kazan in the middle of November, as soon as the snow made traveling possible. My mother settled down in the town, installed her sisters in our house, and made acquaintance with the best society of the place; then she paid visits and received them, took her sisters out to balls and parties, and gave small parties and dinners at home. I pass rapidly over this, and indeed I paid little attention to it all; but I remember how one of these dinners was interrupted by the arrival from Moscow of our first Governess, an elderly French lady, called Mme. Foissier. She flew straight into the dining room and began to complain of the cabman, and we were all taken aback, because none of us could speak French and she knew no Russian.

The year 1807 began. Russia was now definitely at war with Napoleon. A militia was enrolled for the first time in our history; young men crowded into the army, and some of the students, especially the pensioners, asked permission of the Government to leave the University for active service against the enemy; among these were my friend, Panayev, and his elder brother, Ivan, our lyric poet. I blush to confess that I never thought at that time of "rushing, sword in hand, to join the fray"; but the senior Government scholars, who were all destined to enter the teaching profession a year later, were burning to join the ranks of our armies; the career of learned activity, to which they had voluntarily devoted their lives, suddenly became distasteful to them. They were required to serve six years in that profession, and now the obligation seemed an intolerable burden. Contrary to all expectation, their eager desire was very soon granted, and scholars were permitted to enter the army. This happened after I had left college. Science lost in this way many remarkable men, and only a few remained faithful to their former calling. Many received commissions in the artillery, and almost all of these met with an early death.

In January 1807 I sent a petition for leave to retire from the University and enter the civil service. I ceased to attend lectures after this, but I went to college daily and spent all the time of recreation in eager and animated conversation with my companions. Sometimes we played scenes from Schiller's *Robbers*: "Karl Moor" tied himself to a pillar, to serve for a tree, and declaimed the fiery rhetoric of Schiller's young days; then he was released from his tree by "Schweitzer," and all the band of robbers loudly swore to die with their chief.

In March I received my leaving certificate, which, to tell the truth, I did not deserve. Of scientific knowledge I carried away little from the University, not because it was new and small and insufficiently organized, but because I was too young and childish and was drawn aside by my impetuous nature into one hobby after another. Throughout my life I have suffered from a lack of scientific information and solid learning, and this deficiency has been a great hindrance to me both in my profession and in my pursuit of literature.

The day for my departure was fixed; and on the previous day I went to say a last farewell to the University and my companions. Walking in a long chain, arm-in-arm, we visited all the dormitories, lecture halls, and public rooms. Then followed a long and close embrace with each. To take a final farewell, a crowd of students and even of schoolboys poured forth and escorted me to the outside staircase; I went slowly down the steps with a heavy heart; I turned round for one more glimpse of my friends and of the building, and then I made off almost at a run, while the sound of familiar voices rose behind me—"Good-bye, Aksakov, good-bye!"

And I too say good-bye to that season of youthful noise and youthful study, to those early irrevocable years when the blood may be hot and the judgment unripe, but men can hear the voice of honor and follow unselfish aims. That brightness has not yet been clouded over by the claims of society or the petty cares of domestic life. The walls of the school and University and my companions—these made up a whole world to me. There, the problems that puzzle young minds were solved; there, ideals were realized and emotions satisfied. Judgment was passed there, and condemnation or triumphant acquittal pronounced. The rule of the place was complete contempt for all baseness and meanness, for all worldly wisdom and selfish aims, and hearty respect for every high and honorable ideal, however visionary. The memory of years so spent accompanies a man through life; unfelt by him, it lights and directs his path to the very end; and even if circumstances drag him into slippery paths and miry ways, that memory restores him to the high road of truth and honor. I at least, for all of good that survives within me, count myself indebted to the public education of my school and University, and to the stimulus which I carried away with me when I left them. I am convinced that a man who was never at school or University is a defective man, that his life is incomplete, and that he lacks a kind of experience which must be felt in youth or never.

Just before the snow melted in spring, we traveled to Aksakovo, and there I found spring and outdoor sports. Nature was awaking from her winter sleep, and the migratory birds were returning. It was the first time I had really seen and really felt that season; and the effect was to banish from my head for a time all thoughts either of the war with Napoleon or of the University and the companions I had left there.